# Study Skills in English

## Tutor's Book

*Michael J. Wallace*

CAMBRIDGE
UNIVERSITY PRESS

Published by the Press Syndicate of the University of Cambridge
The Pitt Building, Trumpington Street, Cambridge CB2 1RP
40 West 20th Street, New York, NY 10011-4211 USA
10 Stamford Road, Oakleigh, Melbourne 3166, Australia

© Cambridge University Press 1980

First published 1980
Eighth printing 1995

Printed in Great Britain
by Athenæum Press Ltd, Gateshead, Tyne & Wear

ISBN 0 521 22109 9  Tutor's Book
ISBN 0 521 22110 2  Student's Book
ISBN 0 521 22108 0  Cassette

AO

# Contents

# Introduction

The materials in this course have been developed with students attending further and higher education institutions in the U.K., or shortly about to do so.

As everyone teaching such students knows, this group comprises students of widely varying language abilities. To minimise the problem of these different levels, emphasis has been placed on providing a large number of practical exercises, with the linking text kept as brief as possible. This means that

a) the tutor can pitch his explanation of the skill being taught at an appropriate level;

b) the tutor can judge the amount of preparatory work necessary for the exercise to be done successfully.

The exercises themselves have all been tested under classroom conditions and found suitable in a wide range of teaching and learning situations. However, in view of the range of language levels previously referred to, suggestions are made in the Tutor's Book for 'gearing down' various exercises, so that less able students can cope with them. At the other extreme, with very able students, provision of a copy of the Tutor's Book and access to the tape for unit 3 (Taking notes) may enable them to use the course in an autonomous or self-directed way. Some of the exercises in the text itself are self-correcting.

The material for the exercises has been drawn mostly from the social sciences, as a convenient 'half-way house' between arts and science subjects. If at all possible, the students should be further encouraged to relate the skills to their own individual specialisms and course-texts (if the latter are available).

The skills practised are those which relate directly to the needs of most students, namely:

1 How can I read efficiently?   (Unit 2)
2 What is the best method for taking notes?   (Unit 3)
3 How should I prepare myself for seminars and tutorials? (Unit 4)
4 How should I set about researching a major piece of written work?
   How do I organise and present it?   (Units 5, 6 and 7)
5 How should I prepare for examinations?   (Unit 8)

Unit 1 is concerned with the more personal and social aspects of being a student.

Working carefully through the complete course takes about 90 hours, but this could be reduced to 50 or less by a judicious selection of exercises. Quick paths through the units ('Minimum time allocations') are indicated in the appropriate sections of the Tutor's Book.

Alternatively this course can be integrated into other language skills/study skills programmes and used as appropriate. For this reason, each unit has been made as far as possible independent of the other units in the course, although there is inevitably cross-reference from time to time.

In spite of what has been said about the relatively autonomous nature of the units, the tutor might care to note the following recommendations:

Unit 1 (Organising your studies) should be done early in the course but preferably not in the first few hours (see p. 5 below).

Units 5, 6 and 7 (which deal with various aspects of writing an essay) should be done in sequence, if possible.

Unit 8 is written at a somewhat higher level than the rest of the course and should not be tackled at an early stage. On the other hand it need not be left to the very end, especially if the study skills course is a module in the student's full-time course, since it deals in part with matters concerning the student's organisation of his studies.

Of course, there is no reason why units cannot be taught in parallel, for example units 2, 3 and 5 could all be started in the same week.

For a discussion of various aspects of the teaching of Academic English to foreign students, the following book is recommended:

A.P. Cowie and J.B. Heaton (eds): *English for Academic Purposes* (A BAAL/SELMOUS publication. Available from: K.E. Morrow, Centre for Applied Language Studies, University of Reading, Whiteknights, Reading RG6 2AA)

# Unit 1   Organising your studies

(Classtime: 1 hour)

Overseas students coming to Britain face a whole host of problems, some of which are in addition to the normal problems faced by British students. This short unit attempts to bring some of those problems 'into the open' and give the student some guidance as to where he might find help.

Many of these problems are strictly speaking *non-academic*. Yet unless the student is given preliminary advice by someone (and who better than his sympathetic English tutor?), he may not even be aware of who to go to for help. These non-academic problems (often subsumed under the other title of 'culture-shock') have both a *physical* and *mental* side, and very often interact.

Physical problems include the following:

a) *inadequate accommodation*: foreign students often live in cheap flats where there are no facilities for study. If they cannot find (or afford) anything better, then they should at least know about the facilities for study available in college/university/public libraries and lending rooms.

b) they can be adversely affected by the 'strange' *diet* they have to take. The *weather* gets them down (as it can do the natives!). *Travelling* about, even by bus, seems difficult and complicated, especially if their lodgings and halls are away from the city centre. *Money* may be a problem: not always because their grant is insufficient — some students remit an excessive amount of their income home. Budgeting may be a problem, as it is for all students.

Other problems may be more in the mind. *Loneliness* is a great problem. Sometimes it stems from feelings of insecurity and fear of *prejudice*; many students have heard so much about racial prejudice in Britain that they may be apprehensive of being snubbed. Some may have their fears of prejudice confirmed, perhaps in reality, but more often by imagined slights. The natural reserve of British people on buses and trains, for example, can be easily misinterpreted. They may be hurt by the failure of British students to include them in their groups — not realising that some British students are isolated in the same way. Being involved in recreational activities is of course the most obvious way of overcoming this problem.

3

There may also be an *age-gap*. Some overseas students are not only more mature than the undergraduate student population, but may also have held down responsible positions. It is very difficult for them to put themselves in the student situation again. This is one of the reasons that the whole business of assessment is so fraught: such students will have very high expectations, and may be upset by anything less than first-class results.

Others have problems in *life-style*: some (younger) students may over-react to what they see as a very permissive society (and often turns out to be not so permissive as they thought). Married students may miss the comforts of home, and have got out of the way of looking after themselves.

All too often, overseas students who cannot cope with social problems have an excellent excuse to withdraw into isolation, using the pressure of work as their excuse. It is very difficult to get round this since, indeed, they may have academic problems as well.

*Academic problems* may be at two levels. The first level is that of *basic language competence*. The student's command of English may be so poor that he cannot cope in social academic life. Such students may be doomed to fail unless they can be given intensive tuition focussing on basic language skills. It is essential that the language competence of these students is monitored from an early stage, and the application of a standard test at the beginning of the course is recommended.

Most overseas students in Britain, fortunately, have language which is functionally adequate, but which may need improving to cope with the new, more complex demands that will be made of it. These students may be helped by the present course, but may also require further help in certain specific areas.

Linked with this kind of advanced language work is the development of *study skills techniques*, which this course is specifically concerned with. It is to be noted that with overseas students the study skills problem cannot be divorced from the language competence problem, which is why they have been consciously linked in the text. In one sense, the training in study skills is another kind of language practice, and is usually seen by the student himself as more relevant than language work of a more conventional kind, which he relegates to 'school-work'.

## Presentation and organisation

The kind of problems which have been briefly outlined here will be at the back of the tutor's mind as he presents the material in this unit. The basic aim of the unit is to get the student to

4

'externalise' problems (if he has any) and to discuss things (which may be of some anxiety to him) in an objective 'group' way.

*Important*: although this is unit 1 of the course, it should not be done in the first few hours of contact with the students. There are various reasons for this. One obvious one is that if they have just arrived in the U.K. they will not be in a position to discuss whether the points being put forward affect them or not. A second reason is of course that the somewhat 'probing' nature of some of the material demands a more relaxed atmosphere than would be possible at the first few meetings.

The material could be presented after the class has worked with the tutor on some of the other units (e.g. the seminar/discussion unit (unit 4)). Alternatively they can be asked to read through the unit on their own, attempting to answer the questions. The tutor should then

a) perhaps find a chance to go over the questionnaires and personal timetables individually with each student. This would be at the tutor's discretion.

b) in class, discuss the questionnaires and the 'student's survival kit'.

   (i) What do they think of the questionnaires? Do they agree with the answers given by the 'average' successful student? Are all the questions equally important? If not, which are more important?

   (ii) Have they found out the information for the 'student's survival kit'? Are there any gaps which still have to be filled?

   Discussion along these lines can perhaps de-personalise the issues, and allow the students to distance their problems.

### Further reading and teaching aids

There are many organisations in Britain which have much experience in helping overseas students. Probably the best known of these is The British Council which has produced a number of useful publications and teaching aids on this topic. Among these publications is a booklet called *How to Live in Britain* (published by Longman for the British Council). This booklet contains, among much other useful information, a list of addresses of organisations which help overseas students. Similarly helpful, but aimed at those who help overseas students rather than at the students themselves, is the *Overseas Students in Britain Handbook* (published by The British Council, Overseas Students Services Department, 11 Portland Place, London, W1N 4EJ). The British Council has also produced a slide/tape programme for newly-arrived overseas students in Britain called *Making the*

*Most of it* (The British Council, Printing and Publishing Department, 65 Davies St, London, W1Y 2AA).

The United Kingdom Council for Overseas Students Affairs produces *Guidance Leaflets* (enquiries to UKCOSA, 60 Westbourne Grove, London, W2).

The Association of Recognised English Language Schools (ARELS) produces a series of six leaflets with advice and information for students visiting Britain for the first time. They are produced in English and a range of other languages. (Enquiries to: ARELS, 43 Russell Sq, London, WC1B 5DH.)

For an account of the National Foundation for Educational Research in England and Wales (NFER) 1970 survey of overseas students' problems carried out by Amya Sen, see *Students from Overseas* (ed. Alfred Yates) published by the NFER in the 'Exploring Education' series (1971).

# Unit 2 Improving your reading efficiency

This unit concentrates on the following aspects of reading efficiency:

1 The ability to make reading more of an *active* process. The student is encouraged to ask questions before he starts reading a passage, or between surveying the passage and reading it (the 'pre-question technique'). This technique helps concentration (the reading is not aimless) and also memory (the student is relating his reading to his own concerns and interests).

2 The ability to *survey* and *scan* a text, whether it is a book or an article. These techniques save time as they enable the student to locate what is relevant to his interests. They also improve comprehension. Having a general idea of what the text is about means that anticipation is improved, as the reader has a conceptual framework into which he can fit new information.

3 Practice in *reading* and *looking for information under pressure of time*. Many non-native readers, even at advanced level, are very rigid in their speed of reading, being in the habit, very often, of reading everything at the same speed. This kind of inflexibility is very inefficient, but breaking out of it is simply a matter of practice. Therefore, the exercises in this unit are timed wherever this is appropriate.

4 Practice in *abstracting the organisation and main ideas*. This is of course invaluable for general comprehension, note taking and summary. Because of the distracting effect of lexical and idiomatic difficulties, non-native readers often read with too narrow a focus, concentrating on details rather than main points.

5 Practice in *understanding* and *interpreting diagrams*. The unit contains examples of the commonest types of statistical and process diagrams. In some cases, the student has been given an opportunity, also, to produce similar diagrams of his own.

## Length and timing

The unit consists of 25 exercises. The answers to exercises 3, 11, 16 and 17 are given in the Student's Book Appendix, pp. 191–2. The student is also provided with a 'Reading speed table',

7

Appendix, p. 193 for exercises 8, 10, 11 and 14—17. The table covers reading speeds for 80 w.p.m. to 500+ w.p.m.

*Note:* as in all the other units, the assumption is made that all the work is being done in class. Time can be saved, of course, by assigning work to be done outside classtime. In this unit, however, a limiting factor on this might be the necessity for some exercises to be timed.

*Full time allocation: 15 hours*

| | | |
|---|---|---|
| Hour 1 | (Introduction to reading efficiency) | |
| | Reading with a purpose | Exercises 1 and 2 |
| Hour 2 | Using the title | Exercises 3 and 4 |
| Hour 3 | Surveying a book | Exercises 5 and 6 |
| Hour 4 | Surveying a chapter using first lines of paragraphs | Exercises 7—10 |
| Hour 5 | Surveying a chapter using first and last paragraphs | Exercise 11 |
| | Scanning | Exercises 12—13 |
| Hour 6 | Multiple reading skills (including organisation analysis): practice | Exercise 14 |
| Hour 7 | Multiple reading skills: practice | Exercise 15 |
| Hour 8 | Multiple reading skills: practice | Exercise 16 |
| Hour 9 | Multiple reading skills: practice | Exercise 17 |
| Hour 10 | Graphic presentation (table) | Exercise 18 |
| Hour 11 | Graphic presentation (table) | Exercise 19 |
| Hour 12 | Graphic presentation (bar chart) | Exercises 20 and 21 |
| Hour 13 | Graphic presentation (line graph, surface graph, and pie graph) | Exercises 22 and 23 |
| Hour 14 | Graphic presentation (histogram) | Exercise 24 |
| Hour 15 | Graphic presentation (algorithm) | Exercise 25 |

*Minimum time allocation: 9 hours*

| | | |
|---|---|---|
| Hour 1 | (Introduction to reading efficiency) | |
| | Reading with a purpose | Exercises 1 and 2 |
| Hour 2 | Using the title | Exercises 3 and 4 |
| Hour 3 | Surveying a book | Exercises 5 and 6 |
| Hour 4 | Surveying a chapter using first lines of paragraphs | *either* Exercises 7 and 8 *or* 9 and 10 |
| | Surveying a chapter using first and last paragraphs | Exercise 11 |
| | Scanning | Exercise 13 |
| Hour 5 | Multiple reading skills: practice | Exercise 14 |
| Hour 6 | Multiple reading skills: practice | Exercise 16 |

(In the graphic presentation section following, minimum time allocation does

8

not allow for discussion, or for production of graphs in classtime.)

| Hour 7 | Graphic presentation (table, bar chart) | Exercises 18–21 |
| Hour 8 | Graphic presentation (line graph, surface graph, pie graph) | Exercises 22 and 23 |
| Hour 9 | Graphic presentation (histogram, algorithm) | Exercises 24 and 25 |

**Presentation**

Some students may challenge the idea that it is possible to read something more quickly with no diminution of, and perhaps even an increase in, comprehension. They can be referred to the findings of Eric and Manya de Leeuw: *Read Better, Read Faster* (1965), p. 29: a group of ten psychiatrists who started with an average speed of 334 w.p.m. (comprehension 78%) finished with an average speed of 647 w.p.m. (comprehension 85%). Of course, these were medium-fast readers to begin with — the most promising category of students, according to the de Leeuws. They were also native speakers.

With non-native speakers, the same potential for improvement is present, although in my experience not quite so dramatically. The table on p. 10 below shows the results of two reading efficiency courses, each lasting 10 hours (one hour per week for ten weeks). The students read two passages in each hour under timed conditions. Although they were given a certain amount of instruction on reading techniques the main emphasis was simply on reading practice. The text used was Edward Fry: *Reading Faster*, which consists of short passages simplified down to a 2,000-word level (C.U.P. 1963).

The students may want to know what a 'good reading speed' is. It is almost impossible to answer this: so much depends on the nature of the material. Also, the whole point of reading efficiently is that one's speed *varies* according to the nature of the material. Some things have to be read slowly almost word by word (as, say, a problem in mathematics, or a legal document); other materials can be skimmed through. The de Leeuws quote (p. 28) some research done in 1956 by Miss K. Napier and E.F. Hart at North-Western Polytechnic under the auspices of the Department of Scientific and Industrial Research. The average speed of 147 untrained native speakers was 232 w.p.m.; the range went from under 200 w.p.m. to over 400 w.p.m. Over one third of the sample came between 200 and 239 w.p.m. I feel that all one can really say to a foreign learner is that, assuming medium-difficult material, a speed of less than 100 w.p.m. is very slow: it is very doubtful whether students reading at this speed are grasping the essential meaning of medium-difficult

9

## GROUP 1

| Composition of group | No. in group | At beginning of course | | | At end of course | | |
|---|---|---|---|---|---|---|---|
| | | Av. speed | Av. comprehension | Range | Av. speed | Av. comprehension | Range |
| English language teachers at elementary level from both foreign language and second language backgrounds | 10 | 221.3 w.p.m. | 78% | 158–316 w.p.m. | 340.7 w.p.m. | 80% | 180–515 w.p.m. |

Reading speed improvement: +54%
Comprehension improvement: +2%

## GROUP 2

| Composition of group | No. in group | At beginning of course | | | At end of course | | |
|---|---|---|---|---|---|---|---|
| | | Av. speed | Av. comprehension | Range | Av. speed | Av. comprehension | Range |
| School administrators: mostly second language | 14 | 256 w.p.m. | 78.6% | 159–375 w.p.m. | 389.4 w.p.m. | 80.7% | 200–638 w.p.m. |

Reading speed improvement: +52.1%
Comprehension improvement: +2.1%

*Reading efficiency of non-native speakers*

texts. 100—200 w.p.m. is still slow. Any student within this range should be devoting some time to reading improvement. 200—300 w.p.m. is average, and a speed range at which fairly rapid improvement is possible. A speed of over 300 w.p.m. is very satisfactory.

Anyway, too much emphasis can be placed on reading speeds as such. As the de Leeuws point out: 'we have known slower readers who could out-distance faster readers when it came to lengthy articles and books, because of their superior skill in planning and organising' (p. 29).

It must be emphasised that the exercises in this unit do not constitute a faster reading course as such. They are intended to give the student some pointers as to how he can organise his reading more efficiently, and with a greater degree of comprehension. The purpose of the exercises is to make sure that the student can apply the technique. Continued improvement is dependent upon practice with appropriate material. Whether or not the student puts the techniques into practice will probably depend on whether or not he is convinced of the validity of the techniques. (See 'Recommended reading' at the end of this unit commentary, p. 27 below.)

## Reading with a purpose    (Exercises 1 and 2)

This section is concerned with promoting an active attitude to reading. A large variety of responses can be expected. Discussion of alternative suggestions can show how we do not (and should not) usually come to reading with a blank mind. At the same time our pre-conceptions should not be inflexible, so that we are blinded to the writer's point of view.

### Exercise 1

*Answers*

A 1 Encyclopedia articles.
  2 Anything that is handy and not too boring!
  3 Newspapers and magazines.
  4 Prescribed and recommended textbooks.
  5 Atlases, gazetteers and guide-books.

B The difference between A and B is that the reader in A has a purpose in reading (however general) which relates to the kind of text he has chosen. The reasons under B are not nearly so relevant to any particular text. Even if the original motivation is that the book appears on a booklist, the student should try to supply a more specific purpose of his own: 'I want to find out about . . . ' etc.

11

## Exercise 2

*Answers*

1 Lines 50–3: 'Nylon, for example, is a man-made fibre with molecules made out of carbon chains in which atoms of nitrogen, hydrogen, and oxygen fit in a particular arrangement.'
2 Lines 25–6: 'If the carbon chain has hydrogen atoms joined onto it, we have what scientists call a "hydrocarbon".'
3 Lines 7–8: 'Carbon atoms are so special because they have the property of joining together into molecules in different ways.'

## Using the title    (Exercises 3 and 4)

### Exercise 3

The content of the articles is listed in the Student's Book, Appendix, p. 191.
Obviously, the points listed are not 'model answers' but simply an indication of how informative (or otherwise) the title has been.

### Exercise 4

Sample questions might be:
How can we read more efficiently?
What does 'reading efficiently' *mean*?
How can I read faster?
Does reading faster mean understanding less?

It is more difficult to predict what the answers to the questions at the end might be, since they are obviously related to whatever the student put at the beginning. The point is that we cannot predict *everything* that we read — otherwise the information value would be zero. There must be new knowledge, which we have to relate somehow to what we already know.

## Surveying a book    (Exercises 5 and 6)

It would be helpful if the tutor brought along a book which contained most or all of the various reader's aids mentioned in the text, i.e. a blurb, list of contents, publishing details, preface/ foreword and index.

*Blurb* Point out that the purpose of the blurb is to sell the book, so it must be read with caution. Blurbs on academic books, however, are usually fairly straightforward and informative.
   Note that the extracts from reviews are fairly full as such things go, and from very reputable sources.

*List of contents* Note the distinction between small roman numerals for the introductory material, and arabic numerals for the text. The contents list is also a very brief summary of the book.

*Publishing details:*
*Syndic* is the name given to a member of a committee of the Senate of Cambridge University.
© is the symbol of copyright. Copyright means legal protection against a book being published without the copyright owner's permission. Britain is one of the countries which subscribes to the Berne Convention, by which books remain in copyright for fifty years after the death of the author.

*Library of Congress Catalogue Card Number* The Library of Congress is the American equivalent of the British Library. Every book published in the U.S.A. must carry a Library of Congress Catalogue Card Number.

*ISBN* International Standard Book Number. It is used to facilitate the ordering of books. As we can see from the example, each separate *edition* has a new ISBN. The first number identifies the country or group of countries where the book was published, the second group the publisher, the third group the edition, and the fourth is a check number.

*Reprint* means that a new impression of the book has been made with no, or only minor, alterations.

*Edition* A new edition implies that substantive changes have been made in the layout and/or content of a book from a previous edition.

*Photosetting* is a high-speed method of typesetting. It uses a photographic process instead of the more traditional method of typesetting using hot metal.

(For further information on publishing terms, see Henry Jacob: *A Pocket Dictionary of Publishing Terms*, Macdonald and Jane's, London, 1976.)

### Exercise 5

*Answers*

1 He is (or was, at the time of publication) a Senior Lecturer in Sociology at the University of Leeds (see end of section i). Since the book is about Sociology, his position seems to be relevant.
2 It was first published in 1968; there was a second edition in

1974 (see section v). In section iii the author tells us that 'some recent discoveries have made it necessary to modify the approach to important areas of the subject' and that he has had 'the opportunity to carry out a full revision'.

3 In section i — the blurb — we are told that he uses 'appropriate examples of African experience'. At the end of his preface (section iii), he thanks colleagues and students 'here and in Africa'. He almost certainly taught his subject to African students at one time.

4 See the reviews quoted on the blurb (section ii) from reputable journals.

5 a) Yes — see the review from *Sociology* in section ii — 'straightforward conveyance of ideas and information'. Also the *TES* review — 'simple directness and clarity that is difficult in any subject and rare indeed in sociology'.
   b) No; it is continually represented as an introduction to the subject.
   c) Yes — see the review from *The Teacher* (Uganda) — 'A very useful, short introduction . . . '
   d) Yes — see the review from the *TES* — 'a thoroughly sound and authoritative introduction'. Also we know that the author holds an academic position in the subject.
   e) No — it is an introduction. See also the review in *The Teacher* (Uganda) — 'certainly to be recommended to first year students in African universities, and it has been expressly written for them . . . '

6 Part 2, chapter 6. (See section iv, List of contents.)

## Exercise 6

The aims of this are
a) to show the basic use of an index (i.e. locating where topics are referred to in the text).
b) to give some guidelines on more sophisticated use of an index (e.g. where to look for extensive treatment of a topic).
*Note:* in exercises like this, where there is constant reference to a page other than the one on which the exercise is located, it may be a good idea to get the students to work in pairs.

*Answers*

1 a) briefly
  b) briefly
  c) at length
  d) at length
  e) at length

2 a) pp. 169—75
  b) pp. 69—104
  c) pp. 73—84
  d) pp. 126—7 and 141—2

## Surveying a chapter using the first lines of paragraphs
(Exercises 7—10)

In this section we have the first of the timed exercises. If possible, have a stop-clock in a conspicuous position so that students
can check their own time. If this is not possible one can use the
technique suggested by Edward Fry in *Teaching Faster Reading*.
The tutor puts up two columns on the blackboard thus:

| MINS | SECS |
|------|------|
|      | 10   |
|      | 20   |
|      | 30   |
|      | 40   |
|      | 50   |

Using his own watch, he points with a stick or his finger to the
appropriate number of seconds. When one minute has elapsed,
he can put '1' under the minutes column, and continue to
record the seconds. Then '1' is deleted and '2' put up. In this
way, a constant timing is kept. A third possibility is, of course,
for the students to time themselves using their own watches,
although it is worth remembering that, in that case, the watches
must show seconds. Times are given on the reading speed table
(Student's Book, Appendix p. 193) to the nearest ten seconds.

### Exercises 7 and 8

The correct answer is summary 3. If your programme permits
you may like to discuss with the class why surveying a chapter
in this way makes for more efficient reading. One reason is, of
course, that if you have grasped the general drift and intention
of a passage, you can then see how all the 'bits' of the passage
fit together. Like pieces of mosaic, the individual sentences only
show their full meaning when they are related to the total
organisation or context.

### Exercises 9 and 10

*Answers*

c) Tornadoes and d) Hurricanes (3 paragraphs each).

It is only fair to point out to the students that it doesn't
always work out as neatly as this. It is not always the *first* sentence in each paragraph that is the most informative. As they
become more skilled they will be able to pick out the key sentences more easily, wherever they are.

**Surveying a chapter using first and last paragraphs**
(Exercise 11)

### Exercise 11

A new technique is introduced here — looking out for the final 'summarising' paragraph. Again, there is nothing infallible about this technique. It often works, but not always.

*Survey*
Answer to question 'Why does the writer call Malaria a *new* threat?':

Because Malaria germs are developing a resistance to modern drugs, and the mosquitoes themselves are becoming resistant to insecticides. NB: This answer is not given in the Student's Book key, since it is obvious on re-reading.

Answers to the questions at the end of the passage are given in the Student's Book, Appendix p. 192 as follows:
1 draining; covering with oil or detergent
2 getting different varieties to mate (females infertile)
3 using screens and netting; drugs (e.g. quinine); insecticides (e.g. D.D.T.)
4 drugs; insecticides

**Scanning** (Discussion and exercises 12 and 13)

Make sure that the students know the difference between *reading fast* (in which every word is read) and *skimming* (in which sections of the text are left unread). Emphasise the different functions of *surveying* (to get an over-all impression) and *scanning* (to look for particular information which one knows, or suspects, is there).

### Exercise 13

*Answers*

leadership pp. 54, 170–2          Janowitz, M. p. 212
libraries p. 113                         inequality pp. 133–54
household pp. 72–3, 94              Kariba p. 48
Ivory Coast pp. 23, 148

**Multiple reading skills (including organisation analysis): practice**
(Exercises 14–17)

It may be useful to begin by discussing text organisation. If time permits, elicit the organisation of the sample passage 'Malaria —

16

a new threat' (exercise 11), before looking at the analysis of it
on p. 29. It is best always to *elicit* text organisation *orally*.

In the keys which follow the anticipation questions, organisation, analyses and summaries given are suggestions only.
Obviously, other questions, analyses and summaries are possible.

## Exercise 14

*Answers*

3 *Anticipation* questions:
   i)   What are the parts of an ecosystem?
   ii)  How can the parts of an ecosystem affect one another?
   iii) How does the ecosystem of a pond work?

6 *Organisation*
   In this extract an area of study (an ecosystem) is divided into
   its constituent parts, and a description of how the parts interact is given, with examples. It could be represented thus:

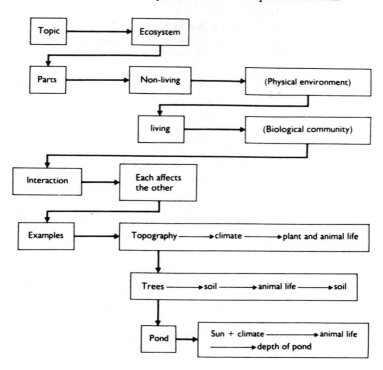

## 7 *Summary*

An ecosystem is made up of two parts: the non-living (physical environment) and the living (biological community).

These two parts affect each other. Thus, the non-living environment determines the kind of life that can exist (e.g. presence or absence of vegetation may depend on topography), but the living biological community can also affect the physical environment (e.g. the presence of living trees maintains the soil).

A small pond is a good example of how an ecosystem works. For example, non-living aspects such as climate etc determine what can live in the pond, but when the living things die they also affect the non-living aspects of the pond by falling to the bottom of it and making it shallower.

## Exercise 15

*Answers*

### 3 *Anticipation*

i) What are 'predators'?

ii) Do parasites or predators have any uses?

iii) What do we mean by 'symbiosis'?

6 *Organisation*

This passage is of a very common type in expository writing where technical terms (*predator, parasite, biological control, symbiosis, mutualism, commensalism*) are defined and exemplified. Note that in the case of *biological control* and *symbiosis* the concept is exemplified before the term is given.

The organisation of this passage could be represented as follows:

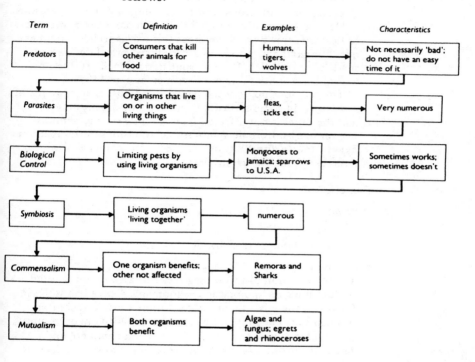

## 7 *Summary*

Living things in an ecosystem affect each other in many ways. Predators are consumers that kill other animals for food. Predators are not necessarily 'bad': humans are the greatest predators! People imagine that predators have an easy time of it, but this is not so: tigers and wolves have difficulty in catching healthy prey.

Parasites are organisms that live on or in other living things. They are very numerous: few living things are free of parasites.

Man has often deliberately brought in parasites or predators to destroy some pest. Sometimes this works well; sometimes not. For example, mongooses introduced into Jamaica and sparrows into U.S.A. both became pests also. Therefore, biological control has to be done with great care.

The relationship between parasite and host is an example of *symbiosis*. In some forms of symbiosis one organism benefits and the other is not affected (*commensalism*) e.g. remoras live on sharks. In some symbiotic relationships both organisms benefit (*mutualism*) e.g. lichens and algae, egrets and rhinoceroses benefit each other.

## Exercise 16

*Answers*

### 2 *Scanning*

a) true  b) false  c) true  d) false  e) false

### 5 *Organisation*

The organisation of this passage reflects a common method of describing technological development. A problem is posed for which there is a theoretical solution. Certain technical problems are encountered but they are eventually overcome. In this case, however, the solution is not a complete one. The text organisation could be represented as in the diagram opposite.

### 6 *Summary*

It has been known for a long time that it should be possible to make artificial diamonds, since diamonds are a form of carbon, a common element. Early attempts were, however, unsuccessful until scientists decided to duplicate the natural conditions of tremendous pressure and heat under which diamonds are made naturally. Even this was found not to be enough, but when a metal catalyst was added, artificial diamonds were made for the first time. Artificial diamonds are like real diamonds in every respect, except that they are quite small and not so beautiful in appearance.

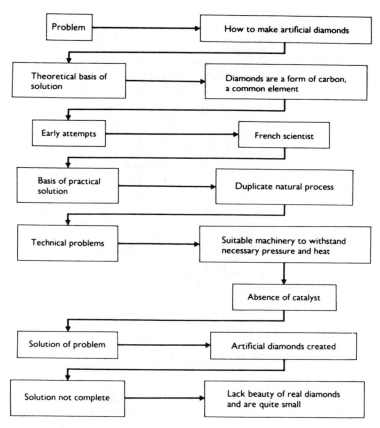

*Exercise 16: text organisation*

## Exercise 17

2 *Scanning*
   a) false  b) false  c) true  d) false  e) true

4 *Organisation*
   This passage has a very common type of organisation. An invention (in this case, the clepsydra or water clock) is described, and various versions of it are listed. Its usefulness is discussed. (In this case, the water clock's advantages *vis-a-vis* the sundial are implied (see *first* paragraph), and its disadvantages are listed.)
   The text organisation could be represented as in the diagram overleaf.

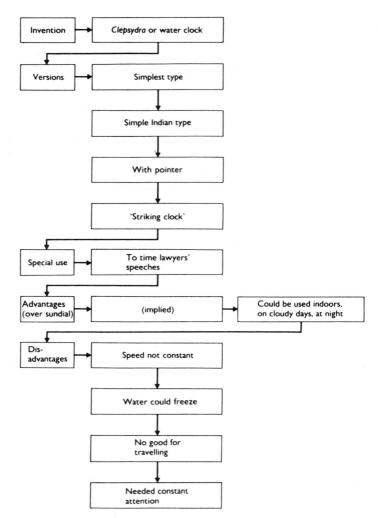

| | | | |
|---|---|---|---|
| Invention | → | *Clepsydra* or water clock | |
| Versions | → | Simplest type | |
| | | Simple Indian type | |
| | | With pointer | |
| | | 'Striking clock' | |
| Special use | → | To time lawyers' speeches | |
| Advantages (over sundial) | → | (implied) | → Could be used indoors, on cloudy days, at night |
| Disadvantages | → | Speed not constant | |
| | | Water could freeze | |
| | | No good for travelling | |
| | | Needed constant attention | |

*Exercise 17: text organisation*

5 *Summary* (Note that the principle of the clepsydra's operation has to be explained.)

An early type of clock that (unlike the sundial) could be used on cloudy days, at night and indoors was the clepsydra or water clock. The simplest type of clepsydra consisted of a bowl with a small hole at the bottom, placed above a larger bowl which marked off into equal parts. Water was poured into the small bowl and dripped slowly into the large bowl. Usually it took an hour for the water to rise from one line to the next in the large bowl. Some clepsydras were much more complicated than this, and there was one that could even strike the hours.

In ancient Greece and Rome clepsydras were used to time lawyers' speeches. They had to stop talking when the clepsydra was empty.

Although the clepsydra had some advantages over the sundial, it also had some disadvantages of its own. The water did not always run out at a constant speed. It could not be used in very cold countries where the water could freeze. It was no good for travellers. It also needed constant attention.

## Understanding graphic presentation   (Exercises 18–25)

Note that, if time is at a premium, this section can be covered more quickly orally and by omitting the discussion and production of graphs.

### Exercise 18

*Answers*

1 Watching television.
2 Swimming.
3 Going for a drive.
4 a) Gardening, car cleaning, playing an instrument, swimming, table tennis, sailing, going for a walk, going out for a meal, attending church.
   b) Watching television, playing with children, home decorations/repairs, going to a pub.
   c) Fishing, going for a drive.
5 Watching television and going for a walk.
6 It is the least of all.
7, 8, 9   (Discussion and research)

### Exercise 19

*Answers*

1 a) delivery; interest; clarity
   b) delivery; clarity; interest
   c) originality; clarity and interest (joint)
2 a) clarity; delivery; notes
   b) delivery and notes (joint); interest
   c) notes; clarity and comprehensibility (joint)
   d) comprehensibility; grasp of subject; clarity

3 The Arts students feature interest and delivery, as well as clarity. The Science students seem to emphasise comprehensibility more.

4 Obviously, many suggestions are possible. One might be that the Science students are depending on the lectures for information, whereas the Arts students are rather seeking stimulus than information.

5 a) Many possible answers. For example, comprehensibility and openness to questioning are rated relatively high at Southampton, and low at Cambridge. Originality is rated very high in Southampton and somewhat lower in Cambridge.

   b) Again, many possibilities. For example, grasp of subject is rated very high at Northampton, and much lower at Cambridge, Leeds and Southampton.

6 Many possible answers. Some of the variations may reflect the smallness of the samples. Something may depend on the teaching methods. If a university has a good tutorial system then 'openness to questioning' during a lecture might not be so important.

7 (Research)

## Exercise 20

*Answers*

1 a) About 24%
  b) About 11%
  c) About 4%

2 Education; Arts generally; Medicine etc; Social, Administrative and Business Studies; Science.

3 Education; Arts generally.

4 Science; Social, Administrative and Business Studies; Engineering and Technology.

5 (Various individual answers)

6 (Discussion)

## Exercise 21

*Answers*

1 Population is much larger in 1974.

2 Older age groups, i.e. 30 years and over.

3 a) Roughly the same number of men and women.
  b) Many more women than men.

4 a) men 6⅔m; women 2½m
  b) men 1m; women 2m

5 a) The 1901 chart shows a much higher proportion of young

24

people. In the 1974 chart, the difference in numbers between the generations is much less marked.

   b) Better protection against diseases; smaller families due to family planning.

6 (Discussion)

## Exercise 22

*Answers*

1  a) 4¼ million.
   b) 10½ million.
   c) Just over 17 million.
2  a) 200,000
   b) 350,000
   c) 330,000
3 1965
4 400,000
5 It remains roughly the same.
6 Until 1964, the number of casualties increased roughly corresponding to the increased number of vehicles; after 1964, the number of vehicles continued to increase, but the number of casualties declined.
7 Various explanations: improved roads; safer cars; regulations about drinking and driving; more safety-conscious public etc.

## Exercise 23

*Answers*

1 Fewer 'Households with head aged 65 or over' than 'All households'.
2  a) Other goods and services; clothing, footwear and durable goods.
   b) Food; housing, fuel, light, power.
3  a) Other goods and services.
   b) Clothing, footwear and durable goods.
4  a) About £10: 24% of £39.43.
   b) About £7: 33% of £21.95.
5 (Discussion)
6 (Research)

## Exercise 24

*Answers*

1 Between 8 and 9 p.m.
2 28%
3 a) Between 2 and 3 p.m.
  b) Between 11 a.m. and noon.
4 a) 2%
  b) 3% maximum
5 11 a.m.—noon; 2 p.m.—5 p.m.; 7 p.m.—10 p.m.
6 'Valleys' can be explained by lunch and dinner breaks (noon—
  2 p.m.; 5 p.m.—7 p.m.) and rest period (10 p.m.—9 a.m.); the
  peak period is in the evening when most students do not have
  classes.
7 Not necessarily. It depends on when their classes are.
8 (Discussion and class research)

## Exercise 25

*Answers (suggestions only)*

1 a) Each step is very clear, and the sequence of steps is clear.
  b) Algorithms may take up more space. They may give
     prominence to information not normally needed. They
     may make it difficult to sort out what is important from
     what is not.
  c) Where a process is very complicated and it has to be
     analysed step by step.
2 Algorithm for *Finding a particular book in the library*. (Title
  of the book is known.)

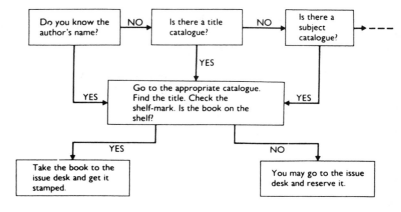

## Recommended reading

For a very informative and readable survey of the psycho-linguistic background to the reading process, see Frank Smith: *Understanding Reading* (Holt, Rinehart & Winston, New York, 1971).

For an account of techniques of teaching faster reading see Edward Fry: *Teaching Faster Reading: a Manual* (Cambridge University Press, 1963). Very practical, although now dated in parts and should be checked against more up-to-date texts, such as Smith's.

It has already been pointed out (p. 11 above) that this unit does not constitute a faster reading course as such. Many such courses are available, e.g.:

Edward Fry: *Reading Faster* (Cambridge University Press, 1963) (Elementary)

Gerald and Vivienne Mosback: *Practical Faster Reading* (Cambridge University Press, 1976) (Upper-intermediate/Advanced)

Eric and Manya de Leeuw: *Read Better, Read Faster* (Penguin Books, Harmondsworth, 1965) (Advanced. Written for native speakers. Also contains material useful to tutors.)

## Unit 3  Taking notes

This unit has three main aims: firstly, to give the student an
opportunity to put note taking in the context of other methods
of acquiring and recording information; secondly, to introduce
some basic techniques of note taking, and thirdly, to give practice
in taking notes from lecturettes. The lecturettes may either be
delivered by the tutor himself or (preferably) from the cassette
tape provided. Exercises 13, 15, 16, 17, 24, 25, 26, 29 and
30 are on tape; they are keyed in the text by the symbol: ⊑▭⊒

### Length and timing

There are 30 exercises.

*Full time allocation: 14 hours*

| | | |
|---|---|---|
| Hour 1 | The aims of note taking | Exercises 1–3 |
| Hour 2 | Taking notes from a text | Exercises 4–5 |
| Hour 3 | Taking notes from a text | Exercises 6–7 |
| Hour 4 | Semantic markers | Exercises 8–10 |
| Hour 5 | Taking notes from a lecture i) Before the lecture | Exercises 11–14 |
| Hour 6 | Taking notes from a lecture ii) The main ideas | Exercises 15–17 |
| Hour 7 | (Correction and discussion) | Exercises 15–17 |
| Hour 8 | Using abbreviations | Exercises 18–20 |
| Hour 9 | Branching notes | Exercises 21–23 |
| Hour 10 | Branching notes | Exercises 24–26 |
| Hour 11 | (Reconstituting notes) | Exercises 25 and 26 |
| Hour 12 | Parts of a lecture | Exercises 27 and 28 |
| Hour 13 | Note taking: practice | Exercises 29 and 30 |
| Hour 14 | (Reconstituting notes: practice) | Exercises 29 and 30 |

*Minimum time allocation: 6 hours*

| | | |
|---|---|---|
| Hour 1 | Taking notes from a text | Exercise 4 |
| | | One of exercises 5, 6 or 7 |
| | Semantic markers | One of exercises 8, 9; or exercise 10, suitably modified |

28

### The aims of note taking   (Exercises 1–3)

The idea of this section is to make the student aware of note taking as one of a variety of methods of acquiring and recording information and to make him aware of the advantages and disadvantages of the various methods. Most of the session will be taken up with class discussion.

### Exercise 1

The purpose of the list is simply to get students thinking flexibly about procedures for recording information.

*Suggested advantages/disadvantages*

| METHOD | ADVANTAGES | DISADVANTAGES |
| --- | --- | --- |
| *Notes taken while listening* | Makes for *positive* note taking. Very good way of integrating new information. | Poor notes may be inadequate and/or misleading. |
| *Notes taken while reading* | Can make reading a more positive process if done thoughtfully and not mechanically. | Danger of passively recording rather than following the thread of the writer's argument. |
| *Notes from memory* | Allows student to concentrate completely on what the speaker/ writer is saying. | Poor recall may result in misleading notes. Important detail may be forgotten. Works better for reading, when one can usually refer back to the text. |
| *Shorthand notes* | Good shorthand notes mean that nearly everything a speaker says can be recorded. | Shorthand has to be learned and requires much practice. Is an 'Automatic' skill (see text). Main points may be lost in detail. |

29

| METHOD | ADVANTAGES | DISADVANTAGES |
|---|---|---|
| *Tape recording* | Good recording means that everything the speaker says is recorded. Student can concentrate on what the speaker is saying without note taking. | Not convenient for revision (unless notes are taken from the recording). May result in passive listening. |
| *Photocopying* | A way of having key articles etc. available for constant reference. May save the tedious copying of long passages (if that is necessary). | Requires photocopying facilities; can be expensive. Possession of photocopies is not a substitute for studying them! |
| *Underlining etc* | If you have a text which has to be thoroughly studied, marking it by underlining etc. can help you find your way round it. | Not possible with library or borrowed books. Making marks on a text is too easy: it can give the *illusion* of study. |

*Other discussion points*

Are there any other ways of recording information that you know about?

How is information recorded in business? At an important meeting? Should lectures be recorded in the same way?

Are there any methods of recording information available to students now, that were not available, say, fifty years ago? (Various electronic methods — tape-recording, photocopying etc.)

Have these new methods made note taking in the traditional way out-of-date?

**Presentation of the lecturettes**

In most groups, the tutor will find wide variation in the students' ability to handle the lecturette material. The tutor should therefore give careful thought to how the material relates to his students' levels and abilities. The following procedures are recommended. (NB: these procedures would not normally apply to the very brief passages in exercise 15.)

1 Before playing (delivering) the lecturettes, the tutor should make sure that concepts which the lecturettes take for granted (e.g. the functions of trade unions; what computers are) are grasped in general terms by the students. A brief discussion along these lines helps to build up 'anticipation' (see unit 2, exercises 1–4).

2 Except for very advanced students (i.e. almost native speaker standard), each lecturette should be played (read) *twice*.

3 *Advanced students* should attempt to take notes on the first hearing. If possible, the tutor should quickly check the results. On the second playing, they can *either* check their notes *or* try to improve on them, depending on how well they have done.

4 *Intermediate students* should *listen carefully* to the first playing (reading) without attempting to take notes. They take notes on the second hearing.

5 *Weak students* can be allowed to *read the transcript* as they listen to the first playing (reading). They take notes on the second hearing.

6 *Staging.* Another way of simplifying the material for weaker students is to 'stage' it, i.e. stop the tape (delivery) at some natural break and check on the students' progress so far. This can be consolidated by discussion before going on to the next section.

It is very useful for students to see 'model notes' of the lecturettes, although the tutor should emphasise that there is no such thing as a uniquely-correct way of displaying notes. Some suggestions for model notes are made below for exercises 21, 22, 23, 24, 25, 26, 29 and 30; these model notes also appear in the Student's Book Appendix. It is also highly instructive if occasionally a lecturette can be played a *third* time, while the students watch the tutor building up model notes on the blackboard or OHP. (To do this systematically for each lecturette should add almost 3 hours to the full time allocation.)

## Exercises 2 and 3

These exercises are really a continuation of the discussion in exercise 1. Why shouldn't students get all the information they need from books, instead of attending lectures and tutorials? Is there anything that a lecture can do that a book cannot do? What are the limitations of lectures? How can we overcome them?

There are many points which may arise from this kind of discussion. Here are some of them:

*Some advantages of lectures* (i.e. good lectures!)
1 A good lecture can give an overview of complex topics.
2 The student has some kind of personal contact with those who will be assessing him. When he is writing his essay he may have a clearer idea of his 'audience'.
3 Students may have an opportunity to ask questions.
4 Lectures are another kind of 'input', complementing reading.
5 Lectures can be more easily up-dated than books.

*Some disadvantages of lectures*

1 A lot depends on the personality of the lecturer. Some people can make even interesting subjects seem dull (and vice-versa, of course).
2 The student is not in control: an uninformative book may be quickly skimmed through; an uninformative lecture has to be endured.
3 The student cannot control the rate of input — it may be too fast or too slow for various students in the same group.

*Some advantages of books*

1 They are usually fuller than lectures.
2 They can be read and absorbed at one's own pace.
3 Several books may give contrasting opinions.

*Some disadvantages of books*

1 When a student fails to understand a point, he cannot ask the writer questions!
2 It may be difficult for him to know how far various aspects of the subject are relevant to his course. This is especially true at the beginning of the course.
3 A beginner may be easily confused by conflicting statements from various books.

## Taking notes from a text    (Exercises 4—7)

You could start this session by looking at the various methods of listing and numbering shown on pp. 53—4 and comparing them. Which system do the students already use? Is there any reason for one system to be preferred to another? (The decimal system is very often used in official reports, for example, which often have complicated subdivisions.)

### Exercise 4

In spite of the fact that the three main divisions are signalled by the use of capital letters, many students still find this a tricky exercise. If you anticipate problems, it might be an idea to precede the exercise by discussing possible subdivisions and explaining more difficult words, e.g. semaphore.

One possible answer would look like this:

*Communication*

I    NON-ELECTRONIC METHODS
    A    messengers
        1    human messengers
        2    birds as messengers — pigeons

B signals
1 signals that can be seen:
a) smoke-signals
b) lighthouses
c) semaphore
d) handwriting
e) printed books
f) newspapers
2 signals that can be heard:
a) drums
b) horns (motor-horns, fog-horns)

II ELECTRONIC METHODS
A using wires
1 telephones
2 cables
B without using wires
1 radio
2 television
3 radio-telephone
4 cinema

III THE USE OF SATELLITES
A communication satellites
B weather satellites
C navigation satellites

## Exercise 5

*Suggested answer*

*Musical instruments*
1 *Wind* instruments (played by blowing air into them)
a) woodwind
i) flute
ii) clarinet
iii) bassoon
b) brass
i) trumpet
ii) horn
c) other
i) mouth-organ
ii) bagpipes
2 *Percussion* instruments (played by banging or striking)
e.g. drum
3 *Stringed instruments*
a) played by plucking
i) harp

       ii)  guitar
   b)  played with a bow
       i)   violin
       ii)  'cello

## Exercise 6

*Suggested answers*

*Acquiring information*
1  From tutors, by
   a)  lecture
   b)  tutorial
   c)  handouts
2  From 'other experts' by
   a)  reading
   b)  listening to:  i)  radio
                    ii)  cassette recordings
   c)  watching T.V.
3  From fellow students, by
   a)  student-led seminars
   b)  contributions of other students in tutorial
   c)  informal conversation
4  From himself, by
   a)  thinking about his subject, and
   b)  linking together what he has heard and seen

## Exercise 7

*Suggested answers*

1  Things it can do:
   a)  arithmetical functions
   b)  memory
   c)  special purpose (scientific etc.)
   d)  programmable
   e)  print out
2  How easy to use:
   a)  display
       i)  clear
       ii)  bright
   b)  keys
       i)  right size
       ii)  right shape
       iii)  reasonable space between keys
       iv)  one function better
       v)  click

3 Power unit:
   a) mains
   b) battery
      i) ordinary
      ii) 'long-life'
      iii) rechargeable
   c) mains adaptor

## Semantic markers   (Exercises 8–10)

Semantic markers are not the only way of signalling the semantic structure of discourse. Very often the relationship between various parts of discourse is implicit rather than explicit. This being the case, there will probably be some disagreement over what constitutes a 'semantic marker' in a given text.

Nevertheless, these markers are worth dwelling on, since they alert the student to the fact that a semantic structure does exist in discourse, and they should be on the look-out for it.

### Exercise 8

*Answers*

Some markers which might be identified are listed below. (The very frequent connector *and* has been ignored.) The suggested classification for exercise 10 is given in brackets.

| | | |
|---|---|---|
| Paragraph 1: | since | (6) |
| Paragraph 2: | not only . . . but | (1) |
| | since | (2) |
| Paragraph 3: | yet | (4) |
| | because | (2) |
| Paragraph 4: | for instance | (3) |
| | but | (4) |
| Paragraph 5: | then, too | (1) |
| | it may happen that | (3) |
| | but | (4) |
| Paragraph 6: | if . . . then | (2) and (9) |
| | but | (4) |
| | then | (6) |
| Paragraph 7: | in fact | (7; or perhaps a new category: stating that something is true) |
| | when | (6) |
| | then | (6) |
| Paragraph 8: | thus | (2) |

|              | for instance | (3) |
|--------------|--------------|-----|
| Paragraph 9: | finally      | (1) |
|              | if           | (9) |

## Exercise 9

*Answers*

|              |                          |     |
|--------------|--------------------------|-----|
| Paragraph 1: | this means that          | (2) |
|              | let us take the case of  | (3) |
|              | it will be obvious that  | (2) |
|              | unless                   | (9) |
|              | clearly                  | (2) |
|              | in other words           | (8) |
|              | let's say                | (3) |
| Paragraph 2: | obviously                | (2) |
| Paragraph 3: | so                       | (2) |
|              | hence                    | (2) |
|              | it follows that          | (2) |
|              | provided that            | (9) |
|              | therefore                | (2) |
|              | examples . . . are       | (3) |
|              | as one might expect      | (2) |
|              | namely                   | (3) |
|              | firstly/secondly/lastly  | (1) |
|              | that is                  | (8) |
|              | thus                     | (2) |
|              | because                  | (2) |
|              | nevertheless             | (4) |
|              | to take one good example | (3) |

## Exercise 10

See answers to exercises 8 and 9 above.

Note that the classification has deliberately been left open-ended. The main thing is to get the students thinking about this aspect of discourse, not to introduce rigid categories.

### Taking notes from a lecture    i) Before the lecture
(Exercises 11–14)

This section repeats a point made several times in the course — the importance of anticipation. Positive note taking is only possible if the student is on the alert, ready to integrate new information into his existing framework of knowledge.

It would be very useful if the points made here about anticipation are repeated before any note taking session — e.g. before exercises 13, 16, 17, 24, 25, 26, 29 and 30. Once the topic is announced a few questions can be elicited from the students prior to presentation.

## Exercise 11

Possible questions are:

1 (*Man's place in the universe*)
Is the Earth the only part of the Universe capable of supporting life?
How did life originate on Earth?
If Man exhausts the resources of Earth, would it be possible for him to live elsewhere in Space?

2 (*Problems of weather prediction*)
How accurate are long-term weather forecasts?
Is there any possibility of weather prediction becoming more accurate?
What are the limitations on accurate weather prediction?

3 (*If you are ill, it's probably your own fault!*)
How can people improve their own health without using medicines?
How important is diet in good health?
How important is mental attitude in health?

4 (*Sharing the ocean's wealth*)
What kind of wealth is being referred to?
How can it be exploited?
What suggestions has the writer on the subject of territorial disputes?

5 (*Influences on human development*)
How far is human development a matter of heredity or a matter of environment?
What is the most important period in a person's life for his development?
What are the things which influence human development?

6 (*Children and books*)
What is the best way of encouraging children to read?
What type of books do children prefer at various stages of their development?
Why is it important to encourage children to read?

7 (*The family in the twentieth century*)
How has the nature of family life changed in this century?
Have the changes, on the whole, been for the better, or not?
How does the speaker see the family continuing to develop?

8 (*Teenagers and drug-addiction*)
What sort of teenagers turn to drugs?
What can parents do to prevent their children taking drugs?
Are all drugs equally harmful?

37

▣ Exercises 12—14

For these three exercises it would be a very good idea to have some illustrative material to hand, namely: an A4-size loose-leaf binder; some A4-size note paper (ready-punched); and also any other note taking aids you can get hold of, e.g. notebook dividers, clipboard, folders etc.

Start by reading through the section on basic equipment, illustrating as appropriate with any materials you have to hand. Before turning on the tape, ask a few anticipation questions about volcanoes (the topic of exercise 13).

After the lecturette is finished, go over exercise 14. Students should look at the model notes, Appendix p. 196. Show around any examples of good layout etc.

**Taking notes from a lecture    ii) The main ideas**
**(Exercises 15—17)**

Go through the introduction to this section with the students.

▣ Exercise 15

The students have to listen to eight extracts on the tape, and then simply underline the correct answer.

*Answers*

Extract 1 — main point; Extract 2 — example; Extract 3 — digression; Extract 4 — digression; Extract 5 — digression; Extract 6 — main point; Extract 7 — example; Extract 8 — main point.

▣ Exercises 16 and 17

The students have to listen to two lecturettes and pick out *main* and *subordinate* points.

Depending on the background and sophistication of the students, it may be necessary to discuss some of the background with them especially such terms as:

(Exercise 16)    sponsored M.P.s
                 affiliation fees
                 constituency (association)
                 Party Conference
                 legal immunity
                 trade dispute
                 monopoly
(Exercise 17)    Trade Union Congress
                 craft union

opinion poll
demarcation dispute

An alternative solution is to let the students (or the weaker ones) read over the lecturettes before they hear them. You might emphasise that the authors are describing their view of the situation as they saw it in the early 1970s — although the general points are probably still true, there has undoubtedly been an expansion of trade union membership since then.

## Exercise 16

*Answers*

| Main ideas | Subordinate ideas |
|---|---|
| 1 political power | a) sponsored M.P.s in the Labour Party |
| | b) Unions are main source of finance for the Labour Party |
| | c) Unions control most votes at the Labour Party Conference |
| 2 economic power | can take industrial action |
| 3 legal protection | a) protection of labour laws |
| | b) excluded from monopoly laws |

## Exercise 17

*Answers*

| Main ideas | Subordinate ideas |
|---|---|
| 1 disunity — congress cannot enforce decisions | a) quarrels between unions |
| | b) quarrels inside unions |
| 2 incompetence — trade union movement not expanding | a) lack of interest (apathy) |
| | b) lack of finance |
| | c) quality of leadership |
| 3 unpopularity | a) demarcation disputes |
| | b) treatment of individual workers |
| | c) strikes |

## Using abbreviations (Exercises 18—20)

The purpose of this section is to stress the value of using abbreviations of a kind that can be 'retrieved' when reconstructing notes.

### Exercise 18

The answer to this exercise will vary from student to student.

### Exercise 19

*Answer* (there will of course be individual variations)

Pyramid = grave of an Egyptian king of the Old and Middle Kingdoms (i.e. 2680 BC—1567 BC).

Earliest P. built for K. Zoser ('Step P.', sides go up in large steps). 197 ft. high.

Largest P. is one of a gp. of 3 built at GIZA, sth. of Cairo, by the kings of the 4th dynasty (2680 BC—2525 BC).

Called 'Great P.', built by K. Khufu (Gk. = Cheops). The outside of this P. = 2m. + blocks of stone. Av. wt. of each block = 2½ tons.

### Exercise 20

*Answer* (there will of course be individual variations)

Malta = 3 islands (viz. Malta, Gozo, Comino) M. island = 95 sq. m.; Gozo = 26 sq. m.; Comino = 1 sq. m. total area < Isle of Wight (U.K.)

1970, pop. = 322,173. Capital = Valetta. V. has a magnificent harbour. The Maltese have their own language, derived mainly from Arabic, but contains also many Sicilian wds.

Chief products = potatoes, veg., grapes, wheat and barley. M. is a v. imp. shipping centre for the Med. and is of great strategic value.

## Branching notes (Exercises 21—26)

The use of branching notes is one of the most important techniques a student can learn. Essentially, they try to reconstitute the totality of the speaker's thought by showing how his ideas relate to one another. They have the added advantage that the structure of even a badly-presented lecture can be revealed by this flexible technique. For the same reason they are very valuable during discussions and seminars, where ideas very often do not follow one another in a logically ordered fashion.

Mistakes to look out for:

1 students squeeze all the notes into one small part of the page. Perhaps they are afraid they will not get all the information in. Practice and guidance can help them overcome this problem.

2 they tend to turn the page round, so that the script is written at several different angles. They can easily be shown that this is not necessary (see examples which follow).

The 'answers' which follow are all suggestions only: there is scope here for a lot of personal variation. Students must not think that there is only one 'correct' solution.

It has already been suggested that for any kind of note taking practice it is very useful experience for the students to watch the tutor build up model notes on the blackboard or OHP, while the tape recorder is playing again a lecturette that they have already made their own notes on.

# Exercise 21

*Model notes*

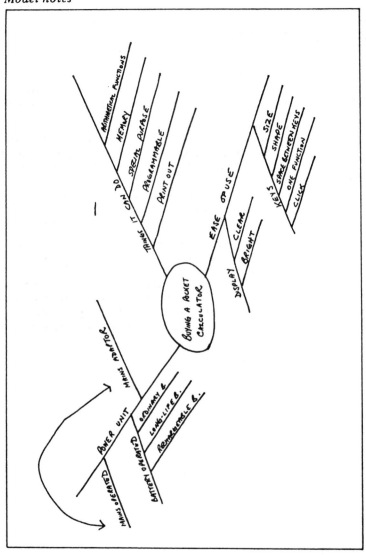

## Exercise 22

*Model notes*

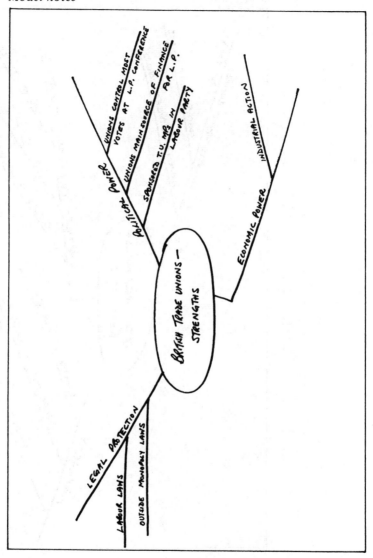

# Exercise 23

*Model notes*

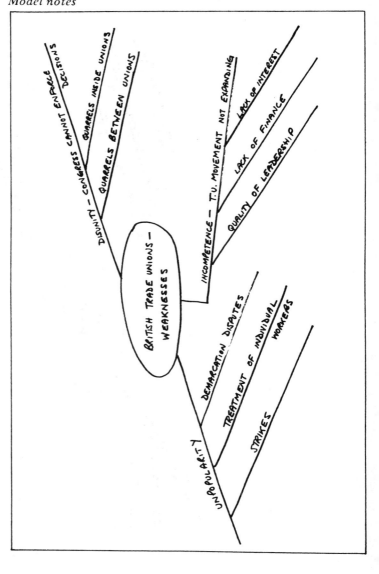

*Model notes*

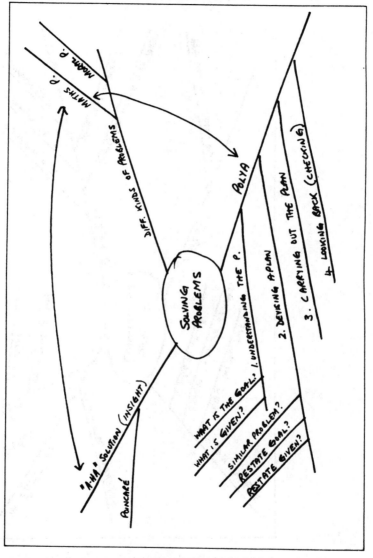

*Note:* the following words may have to be written up on the blackboard and if necessary also explained:
Hamlet (para. 4); A-ha (para. 6); insight (para. 6); Poincaré (para. 7); Polya (para. 9).

*Model notes*

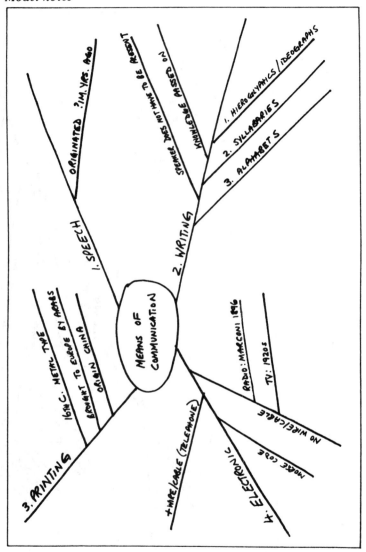

*Note:* the following words may have to be written up on the blackboard and if necessary also explained:
hieroglyphics, ideographs, syllabaries (all para. 4);
Samuel B. Morse, Marconi (both para. 5).

Exercise 26

*Model notes*

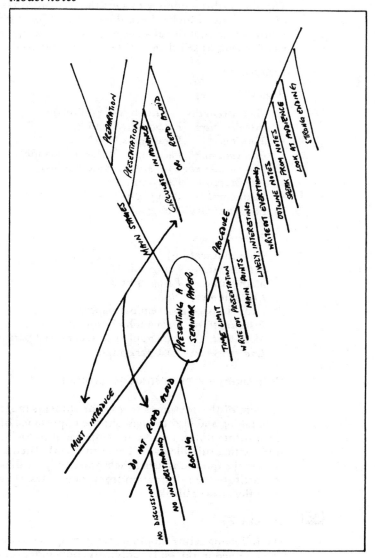

*Note:* the following word should be written up on a blackboard beforehand and if necessary explained:
participants (para. 2).

47

## The parts of a lecture    (Exercises 27—30)

The aim of this section is to alert the student to take advantage of the lecturer who has been thoughtful of his students and has followed the traditional advice: i) tell them what you're going to tell them; ii) tell them; iii) tell them what you've told them.

### Exercise 27

*Answers*

i)  (The strengths of British trade unions)
    *Introduction*    Paragraphs 1 and 2.
    *Main part*    Paragraphs 3—9.
    *End summary* Paragraph 10 (last paragraph).
ii) (The weaknesses of British trade unions)
    *Introduction*    Paragraph 1.
    *Main part*    Paragraphs 2—4.
    *End summary* Paragraph 5.

### Exercise 28

i)  (Communication)
    *Introduction*    Paragraph 1.
    *Main part*    Paragraphs 2—5.
    *End summary* None.
ii) (How to present a seminar paper)
    *Introduction*    Paragraphs 1 and 2.
    *Main part*    Paragraph 3 to second last paragraph.
    *End summary* Last paragraph.

### Note taking and reconstituting: practice

The aim of this section is to give the students more practice in note taking and also to highlight the importance of being able to reconstitute notes. Let the students listen to each lecturette in turn (with a suitable pause between them). Then ask them to answer the questions using their notes only. If they cannot reconstitute the information from their notes, they should leave the answer blank.

### Exercise 29

The following terms should be written up beforehand (they are all explained in the text): polygyny, polyandry, monogamy (para. 3); patrilocal, virilocal, matrilocal, uxorilocal, neolocal (para. 4); bridewealth, dowry (para. 5).

See p. 50 for list notes.

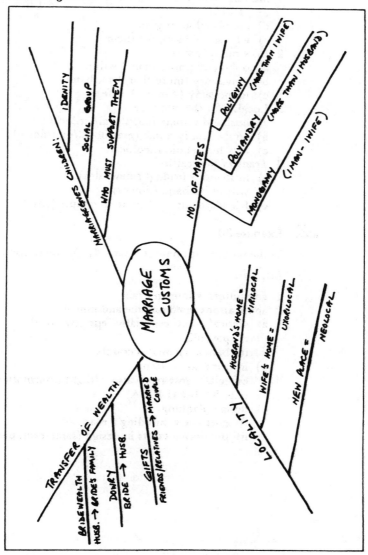

*List notes*

1 Marriage benefits for children
  a) identity
  b) membership of group
  c) who should support them
2 How many mates?
  a) polygyny (more than 1 wife)
  b) polyandry (more than 1 husband)
  c) monogamy (1 man: 1 wife)
3 Locality of the marriage
  a) husband's home (patrilocal/virilocal)
  b) wife's family home (matrilocal/uxorilocal)
  c) new household (neolocal)
4 Transfer of wealth
  a) husband → bride (bridewealth)
  b) wife → husband (dowry)
  c) friends/relatives → married couple (gifts)

**Exercise 30**

To be written up: payroll (para. 3); Boadicea (para. 5).

*List notes*

1 computers ≠ human brain
2 applications in commerce and industry
  a) clerical work, especially repetitive work
      i) payrolls
      ii) banks: clients' accounts
  b) information systems
      especially seat reservations/flight information
      (e.g. BA BOADICEA)
  c) design planning
      i) cost — e.g. building a road
      ii) predicting faults in design (same example)

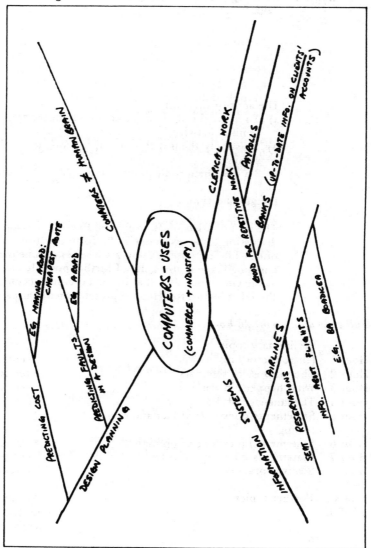

## Recommended reading

For a very stimulating new look at study methods in general, and note-taking procedures in particular, see: Tony Buzan: *Use Your Head* (BBC Publications, London, 1974).

## Unit 4 Taking part in seminars

The aims of this unit are
a) To make the students aware of what precisely is involved in seminar activity.
b) To supply them with some of the interactional tags used in seminars.
c) To give them some practice material to develop seminar skills.

### Length and timing

The unit consists of 30 exercises. Exercise 1 is a preliminary discussion topic; exercises 2–20 form the 'tuition' section of the unit; while exercises 22–30 are a series of nine passages for discussion. There is also a list of further possible discussion topics at the end. Note also, that in the tape that accompanies unit 3, there is a lecturette 'How to present a seminar paper'.

*Full time allocation: 20 hours*

|  |  |  |
|---|---|---|
|  | Preliminary topic |  |
| Hour 1 | (Introductory discussion) | Exercise 1 |
| Hour 2 | The purpose of seminars | Exercises 2 and 3 |
| Hour 3 | What happens in seminars | Exercises 4–8 |
| Hour 4 | The language of discussion | Exercises 9–12 |
| Hour 5 | Statements/questions of fact and personal feeling | Exercises 13–16 |
| Hour 6 | Statements/questions of opinion | Exercises 17–20 |
| Hour 7 | Statements/questions of action | Exercise 21 |
| Hours 8–16 | Seminar practice | Exercises 22–30 |
| Hours 17–20 | Further topics | As suggested at end of unit, or students can suggest their own |

*Minimum time allocation: 10 hours*

|  |  |  |
|---|---|---|
|  | Preliminary topic |  |
| Hour 1 | (Introductory discussion) | Exercise 1 |
| Hour 2 | What happens in seminars | Exercises 4–8 |
| Hour 3 | The language of discussion | Exercises 9–12 |

| Hour 4 | Statements/questions of fact and personal feeling | Exercises 13–16 |
| Hour 5 | Statements/questions of opinion | Exercises 17–20 |
| Hour 6 | Statements/questions of action | Exercise 21 |
| Hours 7–10 | Seminar practice (To be taken from exercises 22–30, or from the topics suggested at the end of the unit, or from topics suggested by the students.) | |

*Note:* It will be noted that the term 'seminar' is used as a shorthand form for any kind of small group discussion.

### Preliminary topic (Exercise 1)

#### Exercise 1

It would be best to start this unit by having at least one informal discussion before commencing the analysis process. For this reason a preliminary topic 'As others see us' has been suggested for the first meeting.

This is a tutor-led topic. The aim is to get the students talking in a context where there is no pressure on any one student. The students should take about five minutes to read the passage silently. Begin with a few comprehension questions to make sure the students have understood the drift of the passage. If there is time at the end, students might consider what someone from Britain would find strange about *their* countries.

### The purpose of seminars (Exercises 2 and 3)

The purpose of this section is to clarify students' ideas about what seminars etc are *for*. For example, if the purpose is to convey factual information, then seminars may be less effective than reading books.

#### Exercises 2 and 3

Some of the reasons for having seminars etc might be:
i) getting a group of people to agree on a common course of action.
ii) giving students a chance to air their views.
iii) affording an opportunity to question a tutor.
iv) training the students to argue and discuss.
v) allowing students to hear and discuss contradictory views.
vi) training students to articulate their views in an intellectual situation.
vii) getting students emotionally and intellectually more involved with their subject.

53

Some uses of lectures:
i) to give an up-to-date survey of a topic.
ii) to stimulate interest.
iii) to clarify a difficult topic.
iv) to give students a chance to 'tune in' to their teachers' way of thinking.

Some uses of private reading:
i) to get information.
ii) to follow the student's own interests.
iii) to give the student a chance to develop his own ideas.
iv) to expand on what he has learnt from lectures etc.
v) to study at the student's own pace.

## What happens in seminars   (Exercises 4—8)

The purpose of this section is to alert individuals and groups to various ways in which discussion can go wrong.

### Exercise 4

*Answers*

1 (P),   2 (P),   3 (N),   4 (P),   5 (N),   6 (P),   7 (N),   8 (N),
9 (P),   10 (N),   11 (P),   12 (P),   13 (N),   14 (P),   15 (N),
16 (N),   17 (P),   18 (P),   19 (N),   20 (N).

### Exercise 5

Answers will depend on individual students. Perhaps this exercise can best be left to be done in the students' own time. It should probably not be 'corrected'.

### Exercise 6

*Answers*

1 (N),   2 (P),   3 (?P),   4 (N),   5 (?P),   6 (?N),   7 (?P),
8 (P),   9 (N),   10 (P).
   Items which are debatable have been indicated with a query (?). Taking item 3, for example, not everybody will agree on the necessity of a timetable for a discussion, and it certainly runs contrary to the traditions of some students, from cultures where everyone is expected to have his say, no matter how long it takes. Even apart from this, other students might debate whether it is feasible to determine beforehand the various stages of a discussion. A lot will depend on the type of discussion being envisaged. The same argument applies to item 5: there seems to be a case for it, but perhaps not in every instance.

Under item 6, it could be argued that note taking destroys the spontaneity and vigour of the discussion. This again may depend on the kinds of notes being taken. Very brief notes on a key issue would presumably do no harm.

## Exercise 7

The answers to this can be a useful commentary on exercise 5. If certain things have been described as positive in exercise 5, and are not true of the 'recent discussion', how important has this been for the quality or effectiveness of the discussion?

## Exercise 8

The answers to this exercise will obviously vary from group to group. Purely as a matter of interest, and *not* as a 'correct' answer, the ranking given by one group who did this exercise was (ranked in order of importance):
  1 − 5 − 2 − 6 − 7 − 4 − 3 − 8
'Extra' suggestions which have been given are:
  9 'It clarifies one's own thoughts.'
10 'It teaches one to be logical.'
(See also suggestions under exercise 1).

## The language of discussion (Exercises 9—12)

The purpose of this section is to bring to the student's attention some useful interactional tags used in discussion.

## Exercise 9

*Answers*

1 Disagree    2 Agree    3 Disagree    4 Don't know    5 Agree
6 Disagree    7 Don't know    8 Agree (in general: disagree on a particular point)    9 Disagree    10 Don't know

## Exercise 10

The purpose of this is to show that the list is not exhaustive. From time to time the tutor may suggest additions to the list which came up naturally in discussion.

## Exercise 11

1 Change your mind    2 Come into the discussion    3 Come into the discussion    4 Change your mind    5 Sum up    6 Sum up    7 Come into the discussion    8 Sum up    9 Come into the discussion    10 Sum up

## Exercise 12

As for exercise 10 above.

## Various kinds of topics   (Exercises 13—20)

The purpose of this section is to distinguish between fact, personal feeling, opinion and action. It will be useful to go over the chart on p. 79 and again at the end before the section on discussion topics, as a kind of summary of the main part of this unit.

## Statements/questions of fact   (Exercises 13 and 14)

### Exercise 13

*Answers*

1 Fact    2 Opinion    3 Opinion    4 Fact    5 Opinion    6 Fact
7 Opinion    8 Opinion    9 Fact (can presumably be verified)
10 Fact (if it can be verified, otherwise merely opinion)

### Exercise 14

When the exercise has been done ask a few students to read aloud their findings. Ask the other students to look out for a) statements of fact; b) other kinds of statements (e.g. opinion). (It may be useful to have the talks taped for reference.)

## Statements/questions of personal feeling   (Exercises 15 and 16)

### Exercise 15

Statements of personal feeling are tricky, because in certain cases it is only possible to discuss them meaningfully if one can agree on appropriate terms of reference. For example, it may be possible to discuss whether 'coffee is a nicer drink than tea' if one can arrive at some definition of 'nice' other than 'it is what pleases me'.

### Exercise 16

This is an apparently simple exercise, but probably some suggestions will come up which have to be discussed, e.g. 'I think the present government is a disgrace', is a debatable statement if the speaker can advance other reasons than personal antipathy to the members of the government.

## Statements/questions of opinion   (Exercises 16—19)

This is the commonest type of discussion topic.

### Exercise 17

*Answers*

1  Is *democracy* the *best* way of running a country?
2  President Kennedy was probably the *greatest* American President of modern times.
3  Scientists should be allowed to perform any kind of experiment they like; otherwise *progress* will come to a halt.
4  In this day and age, no-one can consider himself *truly educated* unless he has studied a *scientific subject.*
5  The urban (city) way of life is obviously an *unnatural* way of life, and that is another reason why country people should be discouraged from moving to the towns.
6  I think that everyone will agree that the first duty of the government is to ensure that every worker gets *a fair wage.*
7  The highest wages ought to be paid to those *who actually do the work* — in other words, the members of *the working class.*
8  Scotland ought to have its *freedom*, like any other *nation.*

### Exercise 18

There are a multitude of answers, e.g. in statement 1, what do we mean by *democracy* — British democracy, American democracy, Russian democracy? What do we mean by *best* — most efficient, fairest, most stable?

### Exercise 19

The answer is in the text.

### Exercise 20

*Suggested answers*

1  Statistics on projections of number of people living in 2000 A.D.; projections on food production by 2000 A.D.
2  Statistics on correlation between incidents of smoking and various diseases, e.g. cancer; number of deaths attributable to smoking.
3  Statistics on number of drivers who die or are injured not wearing seat-belts as opposed to those who died or were killed while wearing them. Statistics on a number of people affected by the kinds of accidents that seat-belts were designed to prevent. How many of those involved were wearing seat-belts?

4 Comparison of murder rates in countries where hanging is the penalty, compared to those where it is not. Comparison of murder rates before and after the abolition of capital punishment. (The somewhat inconclusive nature of this evidence owing to other social and cultural factors can be noted.)
5 Comparison of number of strikes in various trades and professions which have been rated according to some kind of pleasantness/interest scale.
6 Membership of university political parties now and ten years ago; incidence of student disturbance or indiscipline now compared to ten years ago.

## Statements/questions of action   (Exercise 21)

### Exercise 21

*Suggested answers*

1 Problems of existing buildings. Problem of schools outside government control (private schools).
2 Problem of payment for nationalised property. If confiscated, problem of rule of law.
3 Problems of profitability; lack of business knowledge.
4 Problems of enforcing this.
5 Problem of industrial unrest at loss of differentials between trades etc. Problems of motivating workers.
6 Problem of overcoming current enmities. Problem of administration on a global scale.
7 Problem of finding other methods of assessment.
8 Problems of inefficient teaching owing to large classes. Problem of teaching students of widely varying intellect and aptitude.
9 Expense of translating everything into the new language. Problem of training teachers.
10 Problems with trade unions — could cause unemployment. Problem of combining working conditions with security.

## Seminar practice   (Exercises 22—30)

### Exercises 22—30

This section may be used in different ways. It will probably be necessary to be strict with the presenter, so that he does not over-run his time, and also to ensure that he presents *his own views.*

The tutor may chair the discussion himself, or leave it to one of the students. Time spent analysing the discussion is time well

spent. The sort of questions that may be asked at the end are:
Were the terms clearly defined?
Was the topic clearly presented?
What sort of evidence was presented?
Was the discussion informative?
What sort of research would be needed for a really informed
   discussion?
Did the group agree on any conclusions?

## Further topics

These topics are merely suggestions. The sooner the students get
on to topics of their own choosing the better. (This also applies
to the previous section. The material in these two sections is for
the benefit of the tutor if he is dealing with a group which, for
one reason or another, cannot present its own topics.)

## Recommended reading

There is an excellent article by C.M. and T.F. Johns on 'Seminar
discussion strategies' in the *English for Academic Purposes* collection already referred to in the Introduction, p. 2.

   The teaching of discussion techniques in American High
School and College English Programmes is very well established.
A good example is Halbert E. Gulley: *Discussion, Conference and
Group Process* (Holt, Rinehart and Winston, New York, 1963).

   See also the collection of seminar papers issued by the University of London Institute of Education under the title *Varieties
of Group Discussion in University Teaching* (University of
London Institute of Education, May 1972).

   Although it deals with young children in school and is therefore not strictly speaking relevant, nevertheless *Communication
and Learning in Small Groups* by Douglas Barnes and Frankie
Todd is very stimulating and points the way to further research
(Routledge & Kegan Paul, London, 1977).

   Books of the 'conversation' and/or 'discussion' type for overseas students abound and can be found in the catalogues of most
publishers who cater for the EFL market. The use of language
games to promote group interaction and discussion should not
be overlooked.

## Unit 5   Writing an essay   i) Research and using the library

The aim of this unit is to give the student practice in library work and basic research techniques. It will be useful to have a packet of 5" x 3" (127mm x 76mm) cards and 6" x 4" (152mm x 102mm) cards. (They usually come in packets of 100.) Some of the work involves liaison with the library. It would be advisable to know about the classification system used in the library, and also the system of cataloguing.

### Length and timing

The unit consists of 30 exercises. A few of the exercises (e.g. exercise 23) require the resources of a library, but the vast majority do not, and can be used in class.

*Full time allocation: 9 hours*

| | | |
|---|---|---|
| Hour 1 | The importance of essays | Exercise 1 |
| | Systems for tackling essays | Exercises 2 and 3 |
| Hour 2 | Titles and topics | Exercises 4 and 5 |
| Hour 3 | Your own ideas | Exercises 6—8 |
| Hour 4 | Source cards | Exercises 9—13 |
| Hour 5 | Note cards | Exercises 14 and 15 |
| Hour 6 | Finding a book from the library catalogue | Exercises 16 and 17 |
| Hour 7 | Finding a book from the library catalogue | Exercises 18—20 |
| Hour 8 | Finding the book on the shelf | Exercise 21 |
| | Finding your own references (using works of reference) | Exercises 22—25 |
| Hour 9 | Finding your own references (subject indexes) | Exercise 26 |
| | Finding your own references (bibliographies) | Exercises 27—29 |
| | Revision | Exercise 30 |

*Minimum time allocation: 4 hours*

| | | |
|---|---|---|
| Hour 1 | The importance of essays | Exercises 1—8 |
| | Titles and topics | (a quick read through |
| | Your own ideas | sampling the exercises) |
| Hour 2 | Source cards | Exercises 9—11 |
| | Note cards | Exercise 14 |

## The importance of essays   (Exercise 1)

### Exercise 1

The aim of this exercise is to make the student think about the sort of qualities that essays are supposed to reveal; such as evidence of wide reading, ability to relate his reading to a given topic, relevance, originality, evidence of thought etc.

## Systems for tackling essays   (Exercises 2 and 3)

### Exercise 2

The aim of exercise 2 is to give the student an overview of the unit. He has to see that the various sections all have one aim — to enable him to write a good essay.

### Exercise 3

*Suggested answers*

| *General title* | *Specific title* |
|---|---|
| Democracy today | Voting patterns in recent elections |
| Marriage customs | Traditional Christian weddings in Britain |
| The origins of speech | Speech as imitation of natural sounds |
| The development of the aeroplane | The first flight |
| Technology and modern life | How new inventions have helped medicine |
| The Middle Ages in Europe | English medieval literature |
| Rockets and space travel | First journey to the moon |

61

**Titles and topics**  (Exercises 4 and 5)

## Exercise 4

*Suggested answers*

| *General topic* | *Sub-topics* |
|---|---|
| 1 Agriculture and the modern world | a) Mechanised farming<br>b) New methods of production<br>c) Improving the soil<br>d) Distribution of farm produce<br>e) Controlling agricultural pests |
| 2 Education yesterday and today | a) Education in ancient times<br>b) The development of the universities<br>c) Medieval universities<br>d) Education and the professions<br>e) Comprehensive education |
| 3 Advertising | a) T.V. and radio advertising<br>b) Newspaper advertising<br>c) The effects of advertising<br>d) The ethics of advertising<br>e) The cost of advertising |
| 4 The criminal and society | a) Crime detection<br>b) Prison life<br>c) Crime rate and poverty<br>d) Crime and the effects of T.V.<br>e) Re-educating the criminal |

## Exercise 5

Various answers according to individual students.

**Your own ideas**  (Exercises 6–8)

## Exercise 6

*Suggested answers*

| *Yes* | *No* |
|---|---|
| 1 It deters others. | 1 There is a possibility of error which cannot be put right. |
| 2 It is a fitting punishment. | 2 It does not deter others. |
| 3 It satisfies the ordinary | |

people's sense of justice.
4 Murderers who are sent to
prison are generally
imprisoned for life. They
may be difficult prisoners
because no greater punishment can be given to them.

Most murders are thoughtless
crimes of passion.
3 No agency is entitled to
deprive people of life, not
even the State.
4 We should try to re-educate
criminals to play a useful
role in society.

## Exercise 7

*Suggested answers*

1 Statistics on increase or decrease in murder rate in countries
which have abolished capital punishment.
2 Statistics on how many crimes are carefully planned, and how
many are crimes of passion.
3 Data on whether any people hanged for murder have later
been found innocent. Also, how many imprisoned murderers
have later been found innocent?
4 Have any murderers committed a second murder after having
been released for a previous murder?

## Exercise 8

Note that the exercise asks for branching or any other method
of making notes. Although the branching method is undoubtedly
the most efficient for this kind of exercise, list notes are used
here to save space.

*Suggested answers*

1 (The teaching of history in schools)
    types of history:
        political history
        social history
        economic history
    the teaching of world history
    the teaching of national history:
        citizenship
        sense of nationhood
        national bias
2 (Television and juvenile delinquency)
    violence in children's programmes
    how 'real' is T.V. violence to children?
    comparison of violence on different types of programmes
    e.g.
        news programmes

sport (boxing etc.)
adventure
westerns etc.
evidence for effect of T.V. violence on young people
positive uses of T.V. to educate teenagers
3 (Long-term weather prediction)
means of long-term weather prediction:
use of satellites
use of computers
when will it be possible?
implications for mankind:
agriculture
tourism
everyday life.
problems that have to be solved
4 (The usefulness of aid to developing countries)
benefits for giving (donor) countries:
provides new markets
makes for more stable political situations
benefits for receiver countries:
improvements in health, education etc.
chance to modernise
problems:
foreign interference
may damage receiving country's self-reliance and self-
respect
5 (The position of the teacher in society)
teaching as a profession:
financial rewards
social respect
what he teaches:
knowledge?
citizenship?
morality?
discipline in schools and in society
how much control should parents have over the school?
6 (Public law and private morality)
should the law interfere in private morality?
is censorship necessary?
should the law take into account changes in moral
behaviour?
what matters are public and which private:
adultery?
abortion?
should a mistress have the same property rights as a
wife?

7 (The problem of an expanding world population)
    population increase in poorer countries
    will population increase slow down with more prosperity?
    is the present food supply sufficient?
    possibility of expanding the food supply
    religious attitudes
    official action:
        family planning
        voluntary/compulsory sterilisation

8 (Women's liberation)
    means different things in different cultures
    family life and women's lib.
    traditional attitudes
    equal pay
    equal opportunity
    the housewife on a salary?

9 (The United Nations and world peace)
    should there be a U.N. army?
    lack of agreement on fundamental issues
    influence of the major powers
    how far is the U.N. effective as a peacemaker?
    the U.N. as a discussion place
    other ways of achieving peace without the U.N.

10 (Equality of wealth in society — is it possible and is it desirable?)
    what is wealth?
      possessions?
      earnings?
    how can it be re-distributed?
    is confiscation simply legalised theft?
    how would it be handed out?
    is it possible to *keep* people equally wealthy?
    effect on motivation to work hard.

## Source cards  (Exercises 9–13)

In this section each student should have at least nine 5″ x 3″ (127mm x 76mm) cards.

### Exercise 9

*Answer*

```
PHILIP ROBINSON                    (EDUCATION)


            Education and Poverty



Methuen
London,  1976
```

### Exercise 10

*Answer*

```
RONALD STAMPER                    (?BUSINESS
                                    STUDIES)

     Information in Business and Administrative
                      Systems


Batsford
London   1973
```

### Exercise 11

*Answer*

```
J.E. GOLDTHORPE                   (SOCIOLOGY)


          An Introduction to Sociology



Cambridge University Press,
Second edition 1974
```

## Exercise 12

Various answers.

## Exercise 13

Various answers.

## Note cards   (Exercises 14 and 15)

In this section, each student should have two 5″ x 3″ (127mm x 76mm) cards and six 6″ x 4″ (152mm x 102mm) cards.

## Exercise 14

*Answer*

1

```
K.K. BORLAND and                    (?HISTORY)
H.S. SPEICHER


              Clocks, from Shadow to Atom


World's Work Publishers
Tadworth, Surrey 1970
```

2

```
'Until then (i.e. the invention of the hairspring)
watches had been so inaccurate, even as to the
hour, that it was not uncommon for a man to
carry three in order to check one against the
other.'
Borland and Speicher, 1970, pp. 45-7
```

3

'Mary, Queen of Scots, even had a watch shaped
like a skull.   The hinged jaw opened to show
the dial.'

Borland and Speicher, 1970, pp. 45-7

4

B and S emphasise the importance of the
invention of the hairspring.   It was only after
it was invented that watches had minute hands.
Until then watches were so inaccurate that
people sometimes carried three around to check
them against one another.

Borland and Speicher, 1970, pp. 45-7

## Exercise 15

*Answer*

1

MARGARET O. HYDE                    (Geology)

The Earth in Action

Collins
London 1969

2

'. . . there are so many new findings, new
theories, and new methods of learning about
the earth that geology is sometimes thought of
as a science in a state of revolution.'

Hyde, 1969, pp. 50, 51

3

'. . . strong earthquakes are due, mainly, to
the fracturing of great masses of rock many
miles beneath the earth's surface.'
Hyde, 1969, pp. 50, 51

4

H tells us that a <u>tsunami</u> occurs when the
ocean floor suddenly rises or falls.    It is a
kind of earthquake which causes tremendous
waves.    The crests may be as much as 100 miles
apart.

Hyde, 1969, pp. 50, 51

## Finding a book from the library catalogue    (Exercises 16–20)

If you know which library the students are going to be using, it
would be best to find out
a)  what classification system is being used (if it is not the Dewey
    Decimal System, then it would be a good idea for the students
    to get a chance to familiarise themselves with it).
b)  how the cataloguing system works.
In any case, a visit to a library and, if possible, a talk by the
librarian is very desirable.

## Exercise 16

The system by which the boxes work will have to be explained carefully.

*Answers*

| | | | |
|---|---|---|---|
| 1 | KAF – MIK | 6 | CAL – EMB |
| 2 | SIL – ULP | 7 | KAF – MIK |
| 3 | SIL – ULP | 8 | ABB – CAI |
| 4 | ULR – WIM | 9 | WIN – ZYB |
| 5 | GIF – ILE | 10 | GIF – ILE |

## Exercise 17

*Answers*

| | | | |
|---|---|---|---|
| 1 | editor | 4 | Yes |
| 2 | Penguin 1971 | 5 | One |
| 3 | 530 | | |

## Exercise 18

*Answers*

1 George A. Miller
2 150
3 1964
4 Yes – Hutchinson Science Library
5 Yes – it contains a glossary
6 Six

## Exercise 19

*Answers*

| | | |
|---|---|---|
| 1 | Louis MADELIN | 6 |
| 2 | Roger McADAM and David DAVIDSON | 1 |
| 3 | Salvador de MADARIAGA | 4 |
| 4 | Harry Alfred MADDOX | 5 |
| 5 | Thomas Babington MACAULEY | 3 |
| 6 | Rose MACAULEY | 2 |

## Exercise 20

*Answers*

| | | | |
|---|---|---|---|
| 1 | T | 4 | T |
| 2 | C | 5 | I |
| 3 | M | | |

70

**Finding a book on the shelf** (Exercise 21)

See note to previous section.

### Exercise 21

*Answers*

|  |  |  |
|---|---|---|
| 1 | 900—999 | (History) |
| 2 | 400—499 | (Language) |
| 3 | 000—099 | (General, including libraries, etc.) |
| 4 | 200—299 | (Religion) |
| 5 | 700—799 | (Fine Arts) |
| 6 | 100—199 | (Philosophy and Psychology) |
| 7 | 300—399 | (Social Sciences) |
| 8 | 600—699 | (Applied Science and Useful Arts) |
| 9 | 800—899 | (Literature) |
| 10 | 500—599 | (Science) |

**Finding your own references (using works of reference)**
(Exercises 22—25)

### Exercise 22

*Answers*

1 vol. D, p. 12
2 vol. D, pp. 185—6
3 vol. F, p. 89
4 vol. R, p. 175
5 vol. M, p. 819
6 vol. A, p. 90
7 vol. O, pp. 570—1
8 vol. V, p. 334

### Exercise 23

Various answers.

### Exercise 24

*Answers*

1 Reference grammar
2 Dictionary of abbreviations
3 Gazetteer
4 Atlas
5 Yearbook on higher education

6 Biographical dictionary
7 Dictionary of quotations
8 Dictionary of idioms
9 Dictionary of synonyms or *Roget's Thesaurus*
10 *English Duden*

## Exercise 25

1 Technical words, or words used in a technical sense, take the 'foreign' plural, so *bacilli*, *formulae* (mathematics), but *formula* in the general sense becomes *formulas*.
2 WHO: World Health Organisation
3 *City of Montreal*: population 1,197,753 (1971)
4 Ben Nevis is just over 150 miles from Glasgow by road.
5 (Various answers).
6 Born in 1769
7 Mark Twain, American humorist
8 To remain calm
9 Observer; onlooker; looker-on, etc.
10 —

## Finding your own references (subject indexes)   (Exercise 26)

### Exercise 26

*Answers*

| | | |
|---|---|---|
| 1 (secondary schools in Nigeria) | 370.9669 |
| 2 (new towns in Britain) | 711.40942 |
| 3 (Yoruba, language of Nigeria) | 496.3 |
| 4 (refinement of metals) | 622.348 (check under 'nickel') |
| 5 (psychology of sleep) | 154.63 (check under 'night-mares') |

## Finding your own references (bibliographies)
## (Exercises 27–29)

### Exercise 27

Various answers.

### Exercise 28

*Answers*

1 On economic inequality
2 Distribution and measurement of income
3 Amartya Kumar SEN
4 1973 (*delivered* in 1972)

5  Oxford
6  Clarendon Press (Oxford University Press)
7  Yes
8  Yes (from page 107 to page 113)
9  Yes
10  118
11  £2.10
12  £0.90

## Exercise 29

*Answers*

1  Probably a quotation from the publisher's blurb.
2  The reviewer gives three reasons:
   a) the Mariner spacecraft photography.
   b) the charts of the entire surface drawn to a uniform scale.
   c) the succinct introduction to Martian topography.
3  No. The book 'is likely to lead the field for several years'.

## Revision

## Exercise 30

Various answers.

## Recommended reading

See end of tutor's notes on unit 7, p. 87 below.

# Unit 6  Writing an essay  ii) Organisation

The aim of this unit is to introduce the students to various kinds of essay organisation.

## Length and timing

This unit consists of 30 exercises and a glossary of D-words.

*Full time allocation: 18 hours*

| | | |
|---|---|---|
| Hour 1 | Orientation | Exercise 1 |
| | D-words | Exercises 2 and 3 |
| Hour 2 | Listing | Exercises 4 and 5 |
| Hour 3 | Listing | Exercise 6 |
| Hour 4 | Narrative | Exercises 7 and 8 |
| Hour 5 | Narrative | Exercise 9 |
| Hour 6 | Comparison | Exercises 10 and 11 |
| Hour 7 | Static description | Exercises 12 and 13 |
| Hour 8 | Process description | Exercises 14 and 15 |
| Hour 9 | Process description | Exercises 16 and 17 |
| Hour 10 | Process description | Exercise 18 |
| Hour 11 | Cause and effect | Exercise 19 |
| Hour 12 | Definition | Exercises 20–22 |
| Hour 13 | Definition | Exercise 23 |
| Hour 14 | Implication and inference | Exercise 24 |
| Hour 15 | Illustration | Exercises 25 and 26 |
| Hour 16 | Analogy | Exercise 27 |
| Hour 17 | Evidence | Exercises 28 and 29 |
| Hour 18 | Discussion | Exercise 30 |

*Minimum time allocation: 12 hours*

| | | |
|---|---|---|
| Hour 1 | Orientation | Exercise 1 |
| | D-words | Exercises 2 and 3 |
| Hour 2 | Listing | Exercises 4 and 5 |
| Hour 3 | Narrative | Exercises 7 and 8 |
| Hour 4 | Comparison | Exercises 10–11 |
| Hour 5 | Static description | Exercises 12–13 |
| Hour 6 | Process description | Exercises 16–17 |
| Hour 7 | Cause and effect | Exercise 19 |

74

| Hour 8 | Definition | Exercises 20—23 (used selectively) |
| Hour 9 | Implication and inference | Exercise 24 |
| | Illustration | Exercises 25 and 26 |
| Hour 10 | Analogy | Exercise 27 |
| Hour 11 | Evidence | Exercises 28 and 29 |
| Hour 12 | Discussion | Exercise 30 |

## Orientation

### Exercise 1

*Answers*

1 Process description
2 Discussion
3 Comparison
4 Definition
5 Cause and effect
6 Comparison
7 Narrative
8 Process description
9 Static description
10 Cause and effect/illustration

## D-words

### Exercise 2

*Answers*

3 *'Compare and contrast'* : Comparison
4 *'Explain (what is meant by)'* : Definition
5 *'To what extent . . . a product of'* : Cause and effect
6 *'How far . . . a repeat performance'* : Comparison
7 *'trace . . . the development'* : Narrative
8 *'Give an account of the techniques you would use to'* :
   Process description
9 *Describe the layout of* : Static description
10 *Mention some ways . . . can be affected by* : Cause and effect
   *Illustrate* : Illustration

### Exercise 3

Various answers.

## Listing

### Exercise 4

*Answers*

The methods of organisation are: a) by categories and b) in the case of the composers, by order in time.

| | | |
|---|---|---|
| 1 (Instruments) | Piano | |
| | Violin | |
| | Guitar | |
| 2 (Composers) | Mozart | (b. 1756) |
| | Beethoven | (b. 1770) |
| | Chopin | (b. 1810) |
| | Liszt | (b. 1811) |
| 3 (Musical forms) | Opera | |
| | Ballet | |
| | Symphony | |
| | Sonata | |

### Exercise 5

Various answers.

### Exercise 6

Various answers.

## Narrative

### Exercise 7

*Answers*

1  b)
2  a)
3  c)
4  e)
5  g)
6  f)
7  d)

### Exercise 8

Various answers.

### Exercise 9

Various answers.

## Comparison

### Exercise 10

Various answers. What has been done below is to rearrange the various points in a more logical order. Previous order in brackets.

*United Kingdom*

1 Parliament consists of the House of Lords and the House of Commons. (1)
2 The House of Commons is elected at least every five years, sometimes less. (2)
3 The House of Lords is not elected. (4)

4 The Queen is the Head of State. By tradition, she does not interfere in politics. (3)
5 The political leader of the country is the Prime Minister, who is usually also the leader of the largest party in the House of Commons. (7)

6 No written constitution. (5)

7 Judges cannot make constitutional decisions. (6)

*U.S.A.*

1 Congress consists of the Senate and the House of Representatives. (5)
2 The House of Representatives is elected every two years. (7)
3 The Senate consists of 2 senators from every state: one third of the senators are elected every six years. (6)
4 The President is both the political leader and the Head of State. (1)
5 The President is *not* a member of Congress. (2)

6 Congress can refuse to pass bills suggested by the President. (3)
7 The President can veto bills which Congress passes. (4)
8 The Supreme Court (9 judges) interprets the written constitution. (8)

### Exercise 11

Various answers.

## Static description

### Exercise 12

Various answers.

Exercise 13

Various answers.

## Process description

Exercise 14

Various answers.

Exercise 15

Various answers.

Exercise 16

*Answer*

He has ordered his description by, firstly, describing the principles on which cameras work, and, secondly, the functions of the various parts of a box camera.

Exercise 17

*Answer*

The writer has ordered his description by order in time (chronological order).

Exercise 18

Various answers.

## Cause and effect

Exercise 19

*Suggested answers*

1  (For protéction.) Simple cause.
2  (Because of the differing Forces of Gravity.) Simple cause.
3  (Light rays being refracted through drops of water.) Simple cause.
4  (Differing rates at which sea and land cool, with consequent differences in temperature and air pressure.) Simple cause.
5  (Poverty in rural areas, more stimulating life of larger towns etc.) Complex cause.
6  (Popular prejudices against women, women less aggressive etc.) Complex cause.
7  (Scientific research has many effects (either good or bad) in

many areas, such as warfare, medicine etc.) Complex effect.

8 (Effects might be various: loss of inducement to work, strikes by better-paid workers etc.) Complex effect. Also a chain of cause and effect.

9 (Development of popular culture, increased importance of vernacular languages etc.) Complex effect.

10 (Various answers.) Answer depends on the invention, but if it is an important discovery, most probably: Complex effect. Perhaps also chain of cause and effect.

## Definition

### Exercise 20

*Suggested answers*

| A spade | is a tool | used for digging |
| A hammer | is a tool | used for hitting nails etc. |
| A sculptor | is an artist | who shapes solid objects out of stone and other materials. |
| A kitchen | is a room | used for cooking in. |
| A spear | is a weapon | usually thrown at an enemy or stuck into him. |
| A snake | is a reptile | that has no feet and crawls along the ground. |
| A surgeon | is a doctor | who performs operations. |
| A novel | is a kind of writing | that retells imaginary events to achieve an artistic purpose. |

### Exercise 21

*Suggested answers*

| (reptile) | snake, tortoise, lizard . . . |
| (crop) | maize, wheat, rice . . . |
| (mineral) | coal, lead, silver . . . |
| (profession) | doctor, lawyer, teacher . . . |
| (domestic animal) | cat, dog, cow, hen . . . |
| (hobby/pastime) | chess, bridge, stamp-collecting . . . |
| (gem) | diamond, ruby, emerald . . . |
| (traditional custom) | (British custom) fireworks on Guy Fawkes day, dressed-up children visiting houses on Hallowe'en . . . |

## Exercise 22

*Suggested answers*

1 *friend* implies a degree of familiarity and affection that *acquaintance* doesn't.
2 *profession* usually implies some kind of academic qualification, whereas *trade* needn't.
3 *liberty* is a positive thing; *licence* implies too much freedom.
4 *knowledge* means knowing facts; *wisdom* has the sense of knowing the right way to act or to live.
5 *heroism* implies some disregard of danger; *foolhardiness* excessive disregard of danger.
6 *flower* is a type of plant which one wishes to grow for the sake of its appearance; *weed* is a plant which one does not wish to grow.

## Exercise 23

Various answers.

## Implication and inference

### Exercise 24

*Suggested answers*

1 Implies that he, in fact, finds it very difficult to give up smoking. He has tried and failed many times.
2 Implies that people are only interested in their relatives if they are rich.
3 Implies that the man—woman relationship must be a one-sided affair, which works to the advantage of one of the partners.
4 Implies that Art is the product of the individual, whereas Science is a co-operative enterprise.
5 Implies that the law is unjust; it only favours those who are in the wrong.

## Illustration

### Exercise 25

Various answers.

### Exercise 26

Various answers.

## Analogy

### Exercise 27

*Suggested answers*

1. a) The people in a nation have certain things in common (culture, shared experiences, etc.) just as a family does.
   b) The simple structure of family life will not do for a nation.
2. a) Life has 'rules' just like a game.
   b) The 'rules' of life cannot be agreed upon, and may be different for different people.
3. a) Religion may relieve care, as a drug does.
   b) Unlike drugs, religion may bring people into a more self-disciplined way of living.
4. a) Like slaves, workers may have to do work that they do not enjoy.
   b) Unlike slaves, they are paid, and can choose not to work, or to work somewhere else.
5. a) It is literally true that smoke is caused by fire.
   b) The fact that people say a thing does not mean that there is any truth at all in it.
6. a) A democratic government must have a leader (like the captain of a ship).
   b) The decisions about the running of a country usually can and should be taken after long thought; decisions about running a ship have to be taken quickly, so there is usually no time for consultation.

## Evidence

### Exercise 28

*Suggested answers*

1. Put a thermometer in freezing water. (Certain.)
2. Have two groups of people: one which is protected from mosquitoes, the other which is not. Observe the results among those infected by malaria. (Fairly certain.)
3. Give students nonsense sentences to remember, and also the same number of meaningful sentences. See which they remember better. (Fairly certain.)
4. Observe the number of overweight people suffering from heart disease and compare it with the norm of those who are not overweight. (Fairly certain.)
5. Follow the careers of science technology graduates who have become managers or administrators and compare them with

81

the same number of arts graduates in the same kind of career.
(Not very certain. The group may be untypical.)

## Exercise 29

*Answers*

1 Sample too small. (You cannot generalise from one person.)
2 The fact that one thing happens after another does not mean to say that it was caused by it.
3 The fact that two things occur at the same time does not mean to say that they are connected.
4 The sample is not typical. (Obviously people in a choir will be musical.)
5 The sample may be irrelevant. (What is bad for worms is not necessarily bad for human beings.)
6 Irrelevant. (There are different kinds of worms.)
7 The fact that two things occur at the same time (bad air/malaria) does not mean to say that they are connected.
8 The sample is not typical. (Badminton is bound to be popular among badminton players. What do other sportsmen think?)

## Discussion

## Exercise 30

Note: this kind of analysis could be one of the most valuable exercises in the unit. Students should have a chance to practise looking at their arguments with a critical eye.

## Recommended reading

See end of tutor's notes on unit 7, p. 87 below.

# Unit 7   Writing an essay   iii) Presentation

This unit deals with certain aspects of the presentation of an essay, including general layout, sources, references and bibliographies, and correcting a draft. The advice is fairly basic: students at doctorate level, for example, may need the sort of advice given in the books listed at the end for recommended reading.

At certain points (e.g. footnotes, sources and references, list of references) it would be useful if reference could be made to actual textbooks in the students' possession. The use of quotation and reference to support argument could then be analysed in detail in different contexts.

Of course, some departments will have their own regulations about the presentation of essays, in which case the information given in this unit should be modified accordingly.

## Length and timing

This unit consists of 8 exercises.

*Full time allocation: 4 hours*

| Hour 1 | Presentation | Exercises 1 and 2 |
| Hour 2 | Sources and references | Exercise 3 |
| Hour 3 | Footnotes and list of references | Exercises 4 and 5 |
| Hour 4 | Revising the assignment | Exercises 6—8 |

*Minimum time allocation: 3/4 hours*

(Similar to above. But note that exercises 4, 7 and 8 are keyed in the Student's Book Appendix and could be done outside the class.)

## Presentation

### Exercise 1

The object of this exercise is to make the student self-conscious about some very elementary yet often neglected, aspects of presentation.

83

('Pleased'):  Items 3, 6, 10, 11.
('Annoyed'):  Items 1, 2, 4, 5, 7, 8, 9, 12 (perhaps).
('Neither'):  None.

## Exercise 2

The object is to make the student aware of what an abstract is and what sort of information it should contain.

*Answers*

1  The student is not accepting their view, but he is not rejecting it completely.
2  The student is explaining his own point of view.
3  A good summary should contain:
   a)  a brief summary of the argument, or at least the main conclusions.
   b)  a clear statement of the writer's point of view.
4  The summary is one twenty-fifth of the prescribed length of the essay, i.e. it is very brief in comparison to the essay.
5  The advantages of preparing a summary are:
   a)  it gives the reader a good idea of the general drift or direction of the essay. He can therefore read it with greater understanding.
   b)  it ensures that the writer must be clear in his own mind on what he is trying to prove and whether he has succeeded.

## Sources and references  (Exercise 3)

This is a section where it would be beneficial if reference could be made to actual textbooks in the students' possession. The use of quotation and reference to support argument could then be analysed in detail in different contexts.

## Exercise 3

*Answers*

There may be slight variations in presentation.
1  Packard (1960) says this: 'These [the 'real upper class' in the United States] are the people who are likely to be on the board of directors of local industries, banks, universities and community chests; who send their daughters to finishing schools and their sons, probably, to a boarding school and, certainly, to a "good" college.'
   (Alternative: Packard (1960) says of the 'real upper class' in the United States: 'These are the people (etc)'.)

2 Branch and Cash (1966) say this: 'In work with maladjusted children it is necessary to break down the barriers between adults and children.'
3 Barry Commoner (1970) says this: ' . . . the spectacular flights of US astronauts into space — like the similar successes in the USSR — are proof that elaborate achievements in science and engineering not so long ago regarded as impossible have now become matters of routine.'
4 Peter C. Lloyd (1971) says this: 'They [rural primary school leavers in developing countries] . . . move to the town in search of manual or clerical work appropriate, in their own estimation, to their new qualifications.'
(Alternative: Peter C. Lloyd says this of rural primary school leavers in developing countries: 'They . . . move (etc)'.)
5 Nancy Seear (1973) points out that working women are by no means always helped by the attitudes of other working women. The more successful career women enjoy their scarcity value and may not wish to alter this personally satisfying state of affairs.

**Footnotes and references** (Exercises 4 and 5)

Exercise 4

*Answers*

A corrected form of the bibliography is also given in the Student's Book, Appendix, p. 216.
Mistakes:
1 The alphabetical order is wrong (Elliott/Gerstl/Halsey/Jackson/Zander).
2 (Elliott) Name of publisher missing.
3 (Halsey) The initials for Halsey are before the surname, not after it, as in the other examples.
4 (Zander) No publication date.

Exercise 5

Various answers.

## Revising the essay   (Exercises 6–8)

### Exercise 6

*Answer* (Corrected version)

```
Many people say that the 'industrial age' is past
and that we are now in the 'post-industrial age'.
It is said that in the post-industrial age the
capacity to produce has far exceeded the demand
for goods.  Indeed it is true that modern tech-
nology (especially computerisation) ensures that
the ability to produce is limited only by the
supply of materials and energy.

     We can confidently expect that both of these
problems will be overcome in the next century as
synthetic cheap materials are devised and as
renewable fuel resources are developed (e.g. solar
power, nuclear fusion, etc).  Then we can expect
an enormous leap in wealth, and the life-style
enjoyed by only a small elite today will be
accessible to many.
```

### Exercise 7

*Answers*

A full corrected version of this exercise is given in the Student's Book Appendix, p. 216.
1  In paragraph 2, the second and third sentences should be switched.
2  The last sentence in paragraph 2 is irrelevant.
3  The last sentence in paragraph 1 should come at the end of paragraph 3.
4  The fourth paragraph is a conclusion, and should come after the fifth.

### Exercise 8

*Answers*

A full corrected version of this exercise is given in the Student's Book, Appendix, p. 217.
1  Line 3: chatper — chapter
2  *The Ascent of Man* (title)

86

3 sadened — saddened
4 Line 7: question mark at the end of the sentence.
5 In *an* . . . (article omitted)
6 In *the* . . . (article omitted)
7 Line 8: bronowski — Bronowski
8 admit — admits
9 Line 13: ragne — range
10 Lines 13—14: (word order) in order to make more significant discoveries.

## Recommended reading

Books which cover the whole process of writing a dissertation are:

C.J. Parsons: *Theses and Project Work* (Allen and Unwin, London, 1973)

Donald J.D. Mulkerne and Gilbert Kahn: *The Term Paper: Step by Step* (Anchor Books, Doubleday and Co., New York, revised edition 1977)

A book which gives extremely detailed advice on presentation is: Kate L. Turabian: *A Manual for Writers of Term Papers, Theses, and Dissertations* (University of Chicago Press, Chicago and London, 4th ed. 1973).

# Unit 8 Assessment, study techniques and examinations

The aim of this unit is to build up the student's confidence by giving him helpful routines to follow before examinations. Much of the information in the routines will be particular to individual situations.

## Length and timing

This unit consists of 14 exercises. In addition there are a number of 'routines'.

Because of the nature of this unit it is not possible to make any significant difference between a full time and a minimum time allocation.

*Time allocation*

| | | |
|---|---|---|
| Hour 1 | Necessary information about assessment | Exercises 1—3 |
| Hour 2 | Study and memorisation techniques | Exercises 4—6 |
| Hour 3 | Study and memorisation techniques | Exercises 7—11 |
| Hour 4 | Study and memorisation techniques | Exercise 12 |
| Hour 5 | Before the examination | Exercises 13 and 14 |

## Necessary information about assessment (Exercises 1—3)

### Exercise 1

*Answers*

1 The Statistics examination is worth 20% of the total assessment.
2 No. 40% of the assessment is for class tests and 40% for the project.
3 The examination in Economics is much more important — it is worth 60% of the assessment.
4 Yes. At the end of February and June. (Economics essay 20/2; Economic History essay 22/2; Statistics exam on 26/6 and 27/6; Statistics project due in on 21/6; Economics exams on 28/6 and 29/6; Economic History exam on 20/6)
5 Altogether, the exercises are all important: there is no other

assessment. Each individually is worth 4% of the weighting.

6 A pass is not essential in Economic History.

7 Apart from the weekly English exercises and Statistics class tests, no work is due between 22/2 and 20/5, i.e. end February to end May.

8 Probably end of February and June. (See question 4.)

9 Probably the Statistics project could be got out of the way between February and May. Revision for the examinations could be started at end February.

## Exercise 2

*Answers*

1 When the exam is held.
2 What length it is.
3 What kind of exam it is.
4 What the design of the exam is.
5 What areas of the subject it covers.
(Also admissable would be: what weighting it has.)

## Exercise 3

Many overseas students are naive about grades and marks, and over-react to individual grades.

*Answers*

1 There is no way of knowing: we don't know the pass-mark, the average, the range of marks etc.

2 Perhaps not. Grades are by definition less exact than percentage marks.

3 We don't know. (See question 1 above.)

4 He will not necessarily fail Economics. One essay covers only 10% of the assessment. He will not necessarily fail Economic History either, but he is certainly in trouble. The essay carries 50% of the assessment.

5 a) presentation       d) presentation
  b) information        e) information
  c) presentation       f) presentation

## Study and memorisation techniques  (Exercises 4—12)

## Exercise 4

*Answers*

1 *Bill*: 1 hour;   *Jim*: 4 hours.

2 *Bill*: 5 hours;   *Jim*: 20 hours.
3 *Bill*: 200 hours; *Jim*: 800 hours.

## Exercise 5

*Suggested answers*

1 Doing prescribed work.
2 Revision of notes etc.
3 Reading recommended books and articles.
4 Reading books and articles, not recommended, but in the same subject field.
5 Writing model answers for exam questions.
6 Forming a discussion group with a few other interested students.

## Exercise 6

*Answers (approximate)*

1 a) About 35%.
  b) About 30%.
  c) About 27%.
  d) About 23%.
  e) Most forgetting took place immediately after the learning ceased.
  f) We learn that the rate of forgetting is very steep at the beginning and then eases off.
2 a) the A group remembered most.
  b) the E group remembered least.
  c) trying to remember is extremely valuable. It slows down the forgetting process dramatically.
  d) immediately after learning stops.
  e) with each effort to remember the forgetting rate slowed down even more.

## Exercises 7—11

Results will vary according to individual students. We would expect scores to be higher for more meaningful material.

In exercise 11, by adding alternately 3 and 4, starting at the bottom left-hand corner we get this pattern:
5   8   12   15   19   22   26
Continuing at the left-hand side of the top line, we get:
29   33   36   40   43   47

**Exercise 12**

1

---

<u>READING PROCESS AND READING EFFICIENCY</u>

<u>What happens when we read?</u>

    1. R. <u>not</u> a continuous movement : it is SACCADIC
                                   (= jumping).

    2. Eyes move backwards as well as forwards : they REGRESS
                            (NB – <u>not</u> a fault).

<u>Faults in reading.</u>

    1. too SLOW : everything read at same slow speed.

    2. saying words aloud / moving lips.

    3. using a finger or pen to follow.

<u>How to read faster</u> : practice under timed conditions.

    Reading FASTER usually means understanding MORE.

---

2 Various answers.

## Before the examination/During the examination
(Exercises 13 and 14)

The aim of these sections is to help the student partly by helping him to externalise negative attitudes and discussing them in a rational way, and partly by supplying him with the comfort of some practical routines.

### Exercise 13

*Answers*

These comments are suggestions only. There are various possible comments that could be made.

1 This student should discipline himself to follow routines, such as those explained in this unit.
2 This student's behaviour betrays signs of fear and panic. Subconsciously, he possibly feels it all too much for him. Perhaps he should set himself certain minimum tasks which he can easily do, and give himself a deadline to have them finished.
3 These students need help and counselling, they should approach someone who is in a position to help them (tutor, adviser or friend), and seek his or her advice.
4 This student would probably feel better if he discusses his fears with an adviser, tutor etc. He may even need medical help. If the case is not too severe, he can train himself by setting himself 'mock examinations' in his own time, and getting into the habit of quickly jotting down outlines for all the questions he is going to do, before he starts extensive answers.

### Exercise 14

Discussion.

*Routines* It might well be worth going over all the routines and discussing their helpfulness, or otherwise, with the students.

### Recommended reading

For students who wish to do some more reading in this area, the following can be recommended:

Clifford Allen: *Passing Examinations* (Pan Books, London, revised edition 1966)

Christopher Parsons: *How to Study Effectively* (Arrow Books, London, 1976)